A STREETCAR NAMED DESIRE

Tennessee Williams

AUTHORED by Elizabeth Weinbloom
UPDATED AND REVISED by Soman Chainani

COVER DESIGN by Table XI Partners LLC
COVER PHOTO by Olivia Verma and © 2005 GradeSaver, LLC

BOOK DESIGN by Table XI Partners LLC

Published by GradeSaver LLC, www.gradesaver.com

First published in the United States of America by GradeSaver LLC. 2008

ISBN 978-1-60259-145-5

Printed in the United States of America

For other products and additional information please visit http://www.gradesaver.com

Table of Contents

Biography of Williams, Tennessee (1911-1983)....................1

About A Streetcar Named Desire....................5

Character List....................7

Major Themes....................9

Glossary of Terms....................11

Short Summary....................15

Quotes and Analysis....................17

Summary and Analysis of Scene 1....................21

Summary and Analysis of Scene 2....................25

Summary and Analysis of Scene 3....................27

Summary and Analysis of Scene 4....................29

Summary and Analysis of Scene 5....................31

Summary and Analysis of Scene 6....................33

Summary and Analysis of Scenes 7 and 8....................35

Summary and Analysis of Scene 9....................39

Summary and Analysis of Scene 10....................41

Summary and Analysis of Scene 11....................43

Suggested Essay Questions....................45

Music and Streetcar....................49

Author of ClassicNote and Sources....................51

Essay: Chekhov's Influence on the Work of Tennessee Williams....................53

Table of Contents

Essay: Morality and Immorality (The Picture of Dorian Gray and A Streetcar Named Desire)....57

Quiz 1....63

Quiz 1 Answer Key....69

Quiz 2....71

Quiz 2 Answer Key....77

Quiz 3....79

Quiz 3 Answer Key....85

Quiz 4....87

Quiz 4 Answer Key....93

Biography of Williams, Tennessee (1911-1983)

Tennessee Williams was a master playwright of the twentieth century, and his plays A Streetcar Named Desire, The Glass Menagerie, and Cat On A Hot Tin Roof are considered among the finest of the American stage. At their best, his twenty-five full-length plays combined lyrical intensity, haunting loneliness, and hypnotic violence. He is widely considered the greatest Southern playwright and one of the greatest playwrights in the history of American drama.

Born Thomas Lanier Williams on March 26, 1911, he suffered through a difficult and troubling childhood. His father, Cornelius Williams, was a shoe salesman and an emotionally absent parent. He became increasingly abusive as the Williams children grew older. His mother, Edwina, was the daughter of a Southern Episcopal minister and had lived the adolescence and young womanhood of a spoiled Southern belle. Williams was sickly as a child, and his mother was a loving but smothering woman. In 1918 the family moved from Mississippi to St. Louis, and the change from a small provincial town to a big city was very difficult for Williams' mother. The young Williams was also influenced by his older sister Rose's emotional and mental imbalance during their childhood.

In 1929, Williams enrolled in the University of Missouri. After two years his father withdrew him for flunking ROTC, and he took a job at his father's shoe company. He despised the job but worked at the warehouse by day and wrote late into the night. The strain was too much, and in 1935 Williams had a nervous breakdown. He recovered at his grandparents' home in Memphis, and during these years he continued to write. Amateur productions of his early plays were produced in Memphis and St. Louis.

Rose's mental health continued to deteriorate as well. During a fight between Cornelius and Edwina in 1936, Cornelius made a move towards Rose that he claimed was meant to calm her. Rose thought his overtures were sexual and suffered a terrible breakdown. Her parents had her lobotomized shortly afterward.

Williams went back to school and graduated from the University of Iowa in 1938. He then moved to New Orleans, where he began going by the name Tennessee, a nickname he'd been given in college thanks to his southern drawl. After struggling with his sexuality through his youth, he finally entered a new life as a gay man, with a new name, a new home, and a promising new career.

In the early 40s, Williams moved between several cities for different jobs and playwriting classes, also working at MGM as a scriptwriter. In 1944 came the great turning point in his career: *The Glass Menagerie*. First produced in Chicago to great success, the play transferred to Broadway in 1945 and won the NY Critics Circle Award.

While success freed Williams financially, it also made it difficult for him to write. He went to Mexico to work on a play originally titled *The Poker Night.* This play eventually became one of his masterpieces, *A Streetcar Named Desire*. It won Williams a second NY Critics' Circle Award and a Pulitzer Prize in 1947, enabling him to travel and buy a home in Key West as an escape for both relaxation and writing. The year 1951 brought *The Rose Tattoo* and Williams' first Tony award, as well as the successful film adaptation of *A Streetcar Named Desire*, starring Vivian Leigh.

Around this time, Williams met Frank Merlo. The two fell in love, and the young man became Williams' romantic partner until Merlo's untimely death in 1961. He was a steadying influence on Williams, who suffered from depression and lived in fear that he, like his sister Rose, would go insane.

The following years were some of Williams' most productive. His plays were a great success in the United States and abroad, and he was able to write works that were well-received by critics and popular with audiences, including *The Rose Tattoo (1950), Cat on a Hot Tin Roof (1955), Night of the Iguana (1961),* and many others. *Cat on a Hot Tin Roof* won Williams his second Pulitzer Prize, and was his last truly great artistic and commercial success.

He gave American theatergoers unforgettable characters, an incredible vision of life in the South, and a series of powerful portraits of the human condition. He was deeply interested in something he called "poetic realism," namely the use of everyday objects which, seen repeatedly and in the right contexts, become imbued with symbolic meaning. His plays also seemed preoccupied with the extremes of human brutality and sexual behavior: madness, rape, incest, nymphomania, as well as violent and fantastic deaths. Williams himself often commented on the violence in his own work, which to him seemed part of the human condition; he was conscious, also, of the violence in his plays being expressed in a particularly American setting. As with the work of Edward Albee, critics who attacked the "excesses" of Williams' work often were making thinly veiled attacked on his sexuality. Homosexuality was not discussed openly at that time, but in Williams' plays the themes of desire and isolation reveal, among other things, the influence of having grown up gay in a homophobic world.

The sixties brought hard times for Tennessee Williams. He had become dependent on drugs, and the problem only grew worse after the death of Frank Merlo in 1961. Merlo's death from lung cancer sent Williams into a deep depression that lasted ten years. Williams was also insecure about his work, which was sometimes of inconsistent quality, and he was violently jealous of younger playwrights.

His sister Rose was in his thoughts during his later work. The later plays are not considered Williams' best, including the failed *Clothes for a Summer Hotel.* Overwork and drug use continued to take their toll on him, and on February 23, 1983, Williams choked to death on the lid of one of his pill bottles.

He left behind an impressive body of work, including plays that continue to be performed the world over. In his worst work, his writing is melodramatic and overwrought, but at his best Tennessee Williams is a haunting, lyrical, and powerful voice, and one of the most important forces in twentieth-century American drama.

About A Streetcar Named Desire

During the incredibly successful run of *The Glass Menagerie*, theater workmen taught Williams how to play poker. Williams was already beginning to work on a new story, about two Southern belles in a small apartment with a rough crowd of blue-collar men. A poker game played by the men was to be central to the action of the play; eventually, this story evolved into *A Streetcar Named Desire*.

Streetcar hit theaters in 1946. The play cemented William's reputation as one of the greatest American playwrights, winning him a New York's Critics Circle Award and a Pulitzer Prize. Among the play's greatest achievements is the depiction of the psychology of working class characters. In the plays of the period, depictions of working-class life tended to be didactic, with a focus on social commentary or a kind of documentary drama. Williams' play sought to depict working-class characters as psychologically-evolved entities; to some extent, Williams tries to portray these blue-collar characters on their own terms, without romanticizing them.

Tennessee Williams did not express strong admiration for any early American playwrights; his greatest dramatic influence was the brilliant Russian playwright Anton Chekhov. Chekhov, with his elegant juxtaposition of the humorous and the tragic, his lonely characters, and his dark sensibilities, was a powerful inspiration for Tennessee Williams' work. At the same time, Williams' plays are undeniably American in setting and character. Another important influence was the novelist D.H. Lawrence, who offered Williams a depiction of sexuality as a potent force of life; Lawrence is alluded to in *The Glass Menagerie* as one of the writers favored by Tom. The American poet Hart Crane was another important influence on Williams; in Crane's tragic life and death, open homosexuality, and determination to create poetry that did not mimic European sensibilities, Williams found endless inspiration. Williams also belongs to the tradition of great Southern writers who have invigorated literary language with the lyricism of Southern English.

Like Eugene O'Neill, Tennessee Williams wanted to challenge some of the conventions of naturalistic theatre. *Summer and Smoke* (1948), *Camino Real* (1953), and *The Glass Menagerie* (1944), among others, provided some of the early testing ground for Williams' innovations. *The Glass Menagerie* uses music, screen projections, and lighting effects to create the haunting and dream-like atmosphere appropriate for a "memory play." Like Eugene O'Neill's *Emperor Jones* and Arthur Miller's *Death of a Salesman*, Williams' plays explores ways of using the stage to depict the interior life and memories of a character.

In *Streetcar*, stage effects are used to represent Blanche's decent into madness. The maddening polka music, jungle sound effects, and strange shadows help to represent the world as Blanche experiences it. These effects are a departure from the conventions of naturalistic drama, although in this respect *Streetcar* is not as innovative as *The Glass Menagerie*. Nevertheless, *A Streetcar Named Desire* uses these effects to create a highly subjective portrait of the play's central action. On stage, these effects powerfully evoke the terror and isolation of madness.

Character List

Blanche Dubois

Not quite a heroine, Blanche is the complicated protagonist of the play. She is a faded Southern belle without a dime left to her name, after generations of mismanagement led to the loss of the family fortune. Blanche spent the end of her youth watching the older generation of her family die out before losing the DuBois seat at Belle Reve. This experience, along with the suicide of her young homosexual husband, deadened Blanche's emotions and her sense of reality. Desire and death became intricately linked in her life as she led a loose and increasingly careless life, and indeed, after losing her position as a schoolteacher she is forced to depend on the kindness of her one living relation, her sister Stella. Blanche tries to continue being the Southern belle of her youth, but she is too old and has seen too much, and soon her grip on reality begins to slip. She has difficulty understanding the passion in her sister's marriage and is coolly calculating in her relationship with Mitch - yet barely manages to suppress a latent nymphomania.

Stella Kowalski

Stella Kowalski, Blanche's younger sister, is about twenty-five years old and pregnant with her first child. Stella has made a new life for herself in New Orleans and is madly in love with her husband Stanley - their idyllic relationship is steeped in physical passion. Stella is forthright and unapologetic about the nature of her relationship with her husband, and although she loves her sister, she is pragmatic and refuses to let anything come between her and Stanley.

Stanley Kowalski

Stanley Kowalski, Stella's husband, is a man of solid, blue-collar stock - direct, passionate, and often violent. He has no patience for Blanche and the illusions she cherishes. Moreover, he is a controlling and domineering man, demanding subservience from his wife in the belief that his authority is threatened by Blanche's arrival. Blanche, however, sees him as a primitive ape driven only by instinct. In the end, though, Stanley proves he can be as cold and calculating as she is.

Harold "Mitch" Mitchell

One of Stanley's friends. Mitch is as tough and "unrefined" as Stanley. He is an imposing physical specimen, massively built and powerful, but he is also a deeply sensitive and compassionate man. His mother is dying, and this impending loss affects him profoundly. He is attracted to Blanche from the start, and Blanche hopes that he will ask her to marry him. Indeed, Mitch is a fundamentally decent man and seeks only to settle down. But when the truth about Blanche's history comes to light, he feels swindled by her.

Eunice Hubbell

Eunice Hubbell is the owner of the apartment building, and Steve's wife. She is generally helpful, offering Stella and Blanche shelter after Stanley beats Stella. Indeed, she has a personal understanding of the Kowalskis' relationship because it mirrors her own. In the end, she advises Stella that in spite of Blanche's tragedy, life must go on.

Steve Hubbell

Steve Hubbell is Eunice's husband, and owner of the apartment building. As one of the poker players, Steve has the final line of the play. It comes as Blanche is carted off to the asylum and Steve coldly deals another hand.

Pablo Gonzales

Pablo Gonzales is one of the poker players, who punctuates games with Spanish phrases.

Negro Woman

The Negro Woman is a non-naturalistic character; it seems that the actor playing this role is in fact playing a number of different Negro women, all minor characters. Emphasizing the non-naturalistic aspect of the character, in the original production of Streetcar, the "Negro Woman" was played by a male actor.

A Strange Man (The Doctor)

The Doctor arrives at the end to bring Blanche on her "vacation." After the Nurse has pinned her, the Doctor succeeds in calming Blanche. She latches onto him, depending, now and always, "on the kindness of strangers."

A Strange Woman (The Nurse)

The Nurse is a brutal and impersonal character, institutional and severe in an almost stylized fashion. She wrestles Blanche to the ground.

A Young Collector

The Young Collector comes to collect money for the paper. Blanche throws herself at him shamelessly.

A Mexican Woman

The Mexican Woman sells flowers for the dead during the powerful scene when Blanche recounts her fall from grace.

Major Themes

Fantasy/Illusion

Blanche dwells in illusion; fantasy is her primary means of self-defense, both against outside threats and against her own demons. But her deceits carry no trace of malice, but rather they come from her weakness and inability to confront the truth head-on. She is a quixotic figure, seeing the world not as it is but as it ought to be. Fantasy has a liberating magic that protects her from the tragedies she has had to endure. Throughout the play, Blanche's dependence on illusion is contrasted with Stanley's steadfast realism, and in the end it is Stanley and his worldview that win. To survive, Stella must also resort to a kind of illusion, forcing herself to believe that Blanche's accusations against Stanley are false so that she can continue living with her husband.

The Old South and the New South

Stella and Blanche come from a world that is rapidly dying. Belle Reve, their family's ancestral plantation, has been lost, and the two sisters are the last living members of their family and, symbolically, of their old world of cavaliers and cotton fields. Their strain of Old South was not conquered by the march of General Sherman's army, but by the steady march of time, and as Blanche's beauty fades with age so too do these vestiges of that civilization gone with the wind. Blanche attempts to stay back in the past but it is impossible, and Stella only survives by mixing her DuBois blood with the common stock of the Kowalskis; the old South can only live on in a diluted, bastardized form.

Cruelty

The only unforgivable crime, according to Blanche, is deliberate cruelty. This sin is Stanley's specialty. His final assault against Blanche is a merciless attack against an already-beaten foe. Blanche, on the other hand, is dishonest but she never lies out of malice. Her cruelty is unintentional; often, she lies in a vain or misguided effort to please. Throughout the play, we see the full range of cruelty, from Blanche's well-intentioned deceits to Stella self-deceiving treachery to Stanley's deliberate and unchecked malice. In Williams' plays, there are many ways to hurt someone. And some are worse than others.

The Primitive and the Primal

Blanche often speaks of Stanley as ape-like and primitive. Stanley represents a very unrefined manhood, a Romantic idea of man untouched by civilization and its effeminizing influences. His appeal is clear: Stella cannot resist him, and even Blanche, though repulsed, is on some level drawn to him. Stanley's unrefined nature also includes a terrifying amorality. The service of his desire is central to who he is; he has no qualms about driving his sister-in-law to madness, or raping her. In Freudian terms, Stanley is pure id, while Blanche represents the super-ego and Stella the ego – but the balancing between the id and super-ego is not found only in Stella's mediation, but in the tension between these forces within Blanche herself. She finds Stanley's primitivism so threatening precisely because it is something she sees, and hides, within her.

Desire

Closely related to the theme above, desire is the central theme of the play. Blanche seeks to deny it, although we learn later in the play that desire is one of her driving motivations; her desires have caused her to be driven out of town. Physical desire, and not intellectual or spiritual intimacy, is the heart of Stella's and Stanley's relationship, but Williams makes it clear that this does not make their bond any weaker. Desire is also Blanche's undoing, because she cannot find a healthy way of dealing with her natural urges - she is always either trying to suppress them or pursuing them with abandon.

Loneliness

The companion theme to desire is loneliness, and between these two extremes, Blanche is lost. She desperately seeks companionship and protection in the arms of strangers. And she has never recovered from her tragic and consuming love for her first husband. Blanche is in need of a defender. But in New Orleans, she will find instead the predatory and merciless Stanley.

Desire vs Cemeteries / Romance vs Realism

The fundamental tension of the play is this play between the romantic and the realistic, played out in parallel in the pairing of lust and death. Blanche takes the streetcars named Desire and Cemeteries, and like the French's "la petite mort," those cars and the themes they symbolize run together to Blanche's final destination. This dichotomy is present in nearly every element of the play, from the paired characterizations of Blanche the romantic and Stanley the realist, to how all of Blanche's previous sexual encounters are tangled up with death, to the actual names of the streetcars.

Glossary of Terms

amiability
friendly, social

antiquity
from ancient times, a relic

attenuate
to weaken or reduce in force or intensity

bobby-soxer
an adolescent girl, especially in the 1940s

colloquy
a conversational exchange, dialog

coquettish
flirtatious

degenerate
One who has declined in morals and behavior from an acceptable level - in the context of Streetcar, a homosexual

effeminate
having traits generally considered feminine

Elysian Fields
In Greek mythology, the afterworld. Similar in concept to heaven.

gallantry
heroic, courtly attention to women

gossamer
something extremely light, flimsy, or delicate

heterogenous
consisting of dissimilar parts,

hoity toity
assuming airs, pretentious, haughty

hypocritical

pretending to have virtues, morals or principles that one does not actually possess

incongruous

out of place, inconsistent

kibitz

to look on and offer advice

neurasthenic

a person suffering from a psychological disorder characterized by chronic fatigue and weakness, loss of memory, and generalized aches and pains, formerly thought to result from exhaustion of the nervous system. No longer in scientific use.

pinion

to restrain or immobilize a person by holding their arms

portieres

heavy curtains hung across a doorway

Raffish

Gaudily vulgar, cheap, tawdry

redolence

Having a suggestive or reminiscent odor

reproach

blame, censure, disgrace

seven card stud

a variety of poker in which each player is dealt one card face down in each of the first two rounds, one card face up in each of the next four rounds, and one card face down in the last round, each of the last five rounds being followed by a betting interval.

sinuous

having many curves, bends, and turns

sotto voce

without the voice, whispered

swindle

to cheat out of money or other assets

transitory
fleeting, short-lived, non-permanent

vivacity
liveliness, animation, sprightliness

Short Summary

The play takes place right after World War II, in New Orleans, Louisiana.

The Kowalski apartment is in a poor but charming neighborhood in the French Quarter. Stella, twenty-five years old and pregnant, lives with her blue collar husband Stanley Kowalski. It is summertime, and the heat is oppressive. Blanche Dubois, Stella's older sister, arrives unexpectedly, carrying all that she owns. Blanche and Stella have a warm reunion, but Blanche has some bad news: Belle Reve, the family mansion, has been lost. Blanche stayed behind to care for their dying family while Stella left to make a new life for herself, and Blanche is clearly resentful by her sister's abandonment of the family. Blanche meets her sister's husband, Stanley, for the first time, and immediately she feels uncomfortable. We learn that Blanche was once married, when she was very young, but her husband died, leaving her widowed and alone.

Stanley initially distrusts Blanche, thinking that she has cheated Stella out of her share of Belle Reve - but Stanley soon realizes that Blanche is not the swindling type. But the animosity between the two continues. Blanche takes long baths, criticizes the squalor of the apartment, and irritates Stanley. Stanley's roughness bothers Blanche as well, since he makes no effort to be gentle with her. One night, during a poker game, Stanley gets too drunk and beats Stella. The women go to their upstairs neighbors' apartment, but soon Stella returns to Stanley. Blanche is unable to understand Stella and Stanley's powerful (and destructive) physical relationship. That night, she also meets Mitch, prompting an immediate mutual attraction.

The next day, Stanley overhears Blanche saying terrible things about him. From that time on, he devotes himself fully to her destruction. Blanche, herself, has a shady past that she keeps close to the vest. During the last days of Belle Reve, after the mansion was lost, she was exceptionally lonely and turned to strangers for comfort. Her numerous amorous encounters destroyed her reputation in Laurel, leading to the loss of her job as a high school English teacher and her near-expulsion from town.

Tensions build in the apartment throughout the summer. Blanche and Stanley see each other as enemies, and Blanche turns increasingly to alcohol for comfort. Stanley, meanwhile, investigates Blanche's past, and he passes the information about her sexual dalliances on to Mitch. Although Blanche and Mitch had been on track to marry, after he learns the truth, he loses all interest in her. On Blanche's birthday, Mitch stands her up, abandoning her for good. Stanley, meanwhile, caustically presents Blanche with her birthday gift: bus tickets back to Laurel. Blanche is overcome by sickness; she cannot return to Laurel, and Stanley knows it. As Blanche is ill in the bathroom, Stella fights with Stanley over the cruelty of his act. Mid-fight, she tells him to take her to the hospital - the baby is coming.

That night, Blanche packs and drinks. Mitch arrives unexpectedly. He confronts her with the stories of her past, and she tells him, in lurid detail, the truth about her escapades in Laurel. He approaches her, making advances, wanting what she has denied him all summer. She asks him to marry her, and when he refuses, she kicks him out of the apartment.

Hours later, Stanley comes home to get some sleep while Stella's labor continues. Blanche further antagonizes Stanley, destroying his good humor, and he responds by mercilessly destroying Blanche's illusions, one by one, until finally he rapes her.

Weeks later, another poker game is being held at the Kowalski apartment. Blanche has suffered a mental breakdown. She has told Stella about Stanley's assault, but Stella has convinced herself that it cannot be true. A doctor and nurse come and take Blanche away to the asylum. The other men continue their poker game as if nothing has happened.

Quotes and Analysis

I can't stand a naked light bulb, any more than I can a rude remark or a vulgar action. (p. 60)

Blanche

This line clearly sets up the key theme of illusion vs reality. Blanche takes the naked truth - the stark bare lightbulb, the rude remark - and dresses it up prettily to make everyone happier and everything easier. That she speaks of talk and action as analogous to a lightbulb shows that she considers the remedy for uncouth behavior and appearance to be a paper lantern, an external cover, rather than a change from within.

Poker should not be played in a house with women. (p. 63 & 65)

Mitch

During Stanley's tantrum at the poker game, Mitch twice remarks that women and poker are a bad mix. This characterizes Mitch as someone who believes women are soft and gentle and should be protected from the roughness of poker. But it also shows that he doesn't blame the individual - Stanley - for his actions, but instead blames the poker game, as though the testosterone stirred up were unavoidable and necessary.

I'm not in anything I want to get out of. (p. 74)

Stella

This moment represents a major blow to Blanche's world view. Up till now, she was unable to imagine that her sister could be happy with the small flat and the brutish husband. But Stella finally drives home the point that she is not looking for an escape. It crumbles Blanche to learn that this way of life is embraced by someone she loves and respects.

But there are things that happen between a man and a woman in the dark - that sort of make everything else seem - unimportant. (p. 81)

Stella

Stella is explaining her overwhelming love for Stanley in terms of physical passion. Blanche correctly sums this up as "desire," just like "that rattle-trap street-car that bangs through the Quarter." Blanche can recognize desire, but she tries to pretend she can't, and refuses to get on board. She cannot experience desire separately from shame. Stella's contentment with her relationship is completely foreign to Blanche.

I never was hard or self-sufficient enough. When people are soft - soft people have got to shimmer and glow - they've got ot put on soft colors, the colors of butterfly wings, and put a - paper lantern over th elight... It isn't enough to be soft. You've got to be soft and attractive. And I - I'm fading now! I don't know how much longer I can turn the trick. (p. 92)

Blanche

Blanche explains her difficulties in life through a philosophy that pairs softness with attractiveness. She paints herself as floating, without agency or will, just a victim of the demands that the soft be attractive. But the truth is that the abuse of life has forced Blanche to harden up. She resists any hardness, preferring the ephemeral freeness of her youth, and actively undermines any walls and strength that have built up inside her. Her use of the phrase "turn the trick" is also noteworthy, as that is an old idiom for prostitution. Women in Blanche's world view must sell themselves, and when they are no longer a sellable commodity then they are in a desperate situation indeed.

And then the searchlight which had been turned on the world was turned off again and never for one moment since has there been any light that's stronger than this--kitchen--candle. (p. 115)

Blanche

Blanche is telling Mitch the sad details of her marriage to Allan. She loved him truly, despite her disgust at his homosexuality, and something broke inside her when he died. She ties this loss to the theme of light. Blanche hides from bright lights because they expose the truth, but she also avoids them because there is no longer any light inside her to match.

I don't want realism. I want magic! (p. 145)

Blanche

This is Blanche's battle cry. It doesn't matter whether the magic is real. It doesn't even matter whether Blanche herself believes it. What's important for Blanche is that she always have the option of the fantasy - that she can believe in and hope for something prettier and lovelier and kinder than the real world. She is a self-aware Don Quixote, forcing the world to be as beautiful as she imagines it.

Deliberate cruelty is not forgivable. It is the one unforgivable thing in my opinion and it is the one thing of which I have never, never been guilty. (p. 152)

Blanche

Blanche may be deluded about a lot of things, but she is lucid and strong on this point. She lies and cheats and steals, but never to hurt anyone. She wishes only to preserve an illusion. And a fundamental component of her illusion is that she must believe the best of anyone she loves, and believe them incapable of cruelty. She is, unfortunately, unable to make this dream a reality.

We've had this date with each other from the beginning. (p. 162)

Stanley

This is Stanley's implicating moment. In a fundamental way, Blanche and Stanley have always been the only ones who knew what was going on. Blanche knows what part of her story is illusion, and Stanley sees through it all. The conflict of that dynamic was destined, according to Stanley, to come to a head in the bedroom. But this statement also turns Blanche's rape into a premeditated act, turning Blanche for once into as much a victim as she has long painted herself to be.

I couldn't believe her story and go on living with Stanley. (p. 165)

Stella

Stella is the interesting character in the final scene. She has resolved an unresolveable conflict in her soul in the only way possible. Her sister says that Stanley raped her. Stella's only options, therefore, are to either believe Blanche - and leave Stanley - or to consider Blanche's story a lie or a delusion. Even though Stella knows deep down that Blanche was telling at least a partial truth, she must now follow her sister's example and embrace illusion over reality, in order to continue living the life she had before Blanche ever came to New Orleans.

Summary and Analysis of Scene 1

Scene 1:

At rise, we see a two-story building in a poor, charming, diverse section of New Orleans, called Elysian Fields. It is an evening in early May in the 1930s. The Kowalskis live in the downstairs apartment, and Eunice and Steve live upstairs.

The action begins with the arrival of Blanche DuBois, dressed in white, and both looking and feeling entirely out of place on this downtrodden street. Blanche stares at the building in disbelief – her directions brought her to Elysian Fields, but it looks nothing like what she expected. Eunice tells Blanche that she has come to the right place – Blanche's sister, Stella, lives on the first floor. After Eunice lets Blanche into the apartment, she runs around the corner to fetch Stella.

Left alone, Blanche surreptitiously takes a drink of whiskey, and puts the bottle and tumbler away. Stella arrives and they embrace happily, Blanche babbling excitedly about Stella's appearance and not giving her sister a chance to get a word in edge-wise. Stella offers Blanche a drink, which she makes a show of accepting reluctantly. The quality of the neighborhood comes up quickly; Blanche is appalled that Stella is living in such conditions. Stella is perfectly happy with her lot, and doesn't take kindly to Blanche's questions.

As the conversation progresses, it is revealed that Blanche is taking a leave of absence from her position as a school teacher, and plans to stay with Stella for an unspecified period of time. Blanche is concerned about living in such close quarters with Stanley, and makes no effort to hide her discomfort with his blue collar background. Stella is quite in love with her husband, however.

Blanche broaches the subject of the DuBois family plantation, Belle Reve. She is immediately on the defensive as she describes how hard she worked to keep the plantation running, while Stella left to live her own life in New Orleans. A long string of deaths in the family ate up all the money, while the process of nursing dying loved ones took their toll on Blanche's psyche, and in the end Belle Reve was lost. Stella is upset at both the news and the accusatory way Blanche broke it to her, and she goes into the bathroom to cry.

Stanley enters the apartment with Mitch and Steve, all returning from bowling. Blanche hesitantly introduces herself to Stanley, who did not know Blanche was coming to town. He asks Blanche some straight forward questions about herself and her plans, while removing his sweaty shirt and taking a drink. Blanche is appalled. As the scene ends, it is revealed that Blanche was married once, when she was young, but the boy died. The recollection makes her feel sick, and she buries her head in her arms.

Analysis

"They told me to take a street-car named Desire." Blanche's first action in the play is one of confusion, ambivalence, disorientation. She cannot believe where she has ended up, standing at her sister's rundown New Orleans door step, or determine how she got there, on a pair of streetcars named Desire and Cemeteries. Blanche makes it clear from the start that her actions are involuntary – "they," some unknown entity, told her to take a street-car named Desire. This is both meaningful in the present tense and on a deeper thematic level. Blanche is lost; her life is falling apart and she has nowhere to go. Only desperation and a lack of other options has brought her to Elysian Fields, a tenement as different from its heavenly title as can be imagined by Blanche's sheltered mind. And we will learn that throughout Blanche's adult life, without any agency, she has been riding two metaphorical streetcars named Desire and Cemeteries – the dual themes of lust and death that will be paired constantly through the play. Just as circumstance has led her to the Kowalskis' doorstep, so too did circumstance lead her to a life driven by desire and death. The impulses are paired from the very start; which will win?

All of the major themes and elements of A Streetcar Named Desire are introduced as quickly as possible at the top of the play. Tennessee Williams teasingly drops clues about all the major reveals of the second and third acts in the introductory exposition, as though he were writing a mystery. In a way, the play is a mystery, with Stanley investigating Blanche's background and an ever-unraveling layer of truth and un-truth is exposed to the ugly glare of the light. But for now, in the first scene, we only get tantalizing hints as Williams references all the major issues: the loss of Belle Reve; Blanche's drinking; the fear and adoration Stella feels for her husband; Blanche's fear of the light and preoccupation with appearances; the death of Blanche's husband. The second scene brings in the elements particular to Blanche and Stanley's relationship, and from there all the foundation is laid to send the story hurtling down the tracks towards its conclusion.

Williams provides copious stage directions in his plays, and they are both functional and poetic. He does not simply state the necessary movements, nor does he serve as a backseat director, programming every gesture before an actor has touched the text. Rather, his directions are like a depiction of a potential performance – the outline of the Blanche and the Stanley that he sees, but written in gossamer and smoke. For instance, he dictates that Blanche should enter in "a white suit with a fluffy bodice," and further describes her outfit as something appropriate for a cocktail party. But this is not Williams prescribing the elements of what we see, but rather the overall effect – "there is something about her uncertain manner… that suggests a moth." An interesting choice of comparison, as moths are drawn to light the way Blanche is desperately drawn from it.

Also important is the detailed description of the set. We have only one set for the entire play – the crowded apartment of the Kowalskis – but thanks to transparent walls we have access to the street outside as well as the two rooms and bath.

Underscored is the cramped claustrophobia that enters the apartment with Blanche, and the heightened emotions of the bunker as Blanche's hide-out extends longer and longer. The outside world regularly penetrates the apartment, with visits from Mitch and Eunice and the occasional poker night. But rather than letting in air and light, these penetrations just force Blanche to retreat deeper and deeper into her fantasy, hiding from the encroaching walls of the apartment.

But in the first scene, of course, Blanche is still putting on a happy face. She babbles away at Stella, full of chipper gossip and cardboard reminiscences. Blanche deftly deflects any criticism or questioning from her younger sister, and when certain revelations become necessary (as in the telling of the loss of Belle Reve) Blanche succeeds in spinning them around so that she is breaking the news on her own terms. Her defensive strategy is to stay on the offensive – criticizing Stella's lifestyle and social standing when Blanche is in an even worse situation herself, defending herself against blame for the loss of Belle Reve before Stella can even say a word. This Blanche has been twisting and manipulating truths and lies for a long time, and her method seems at first like it will succeed in her new life as well. But then she meets Stanley.

Stanley and Blanche are characterized as polar opposites. He is brutish, coarse, primitive; she is dainty, elegant, delicate. He sizes her up with a glance; she hides her eyes from him. He is direct and blunt; she dances around every topic. But the funny thing about opposites is that they attract. The instant animus between the characters is powerful and binds them together much more so than more positive emotions. This is the beginning that sets up the inevitable date they have with each other.

Summary and Analysis of Scene 2

Scene 2

The next night. While Blanche soaks in a tub, Stella tells Stanley that Belle Reve is lost. She is vague on the details, but Stanley is persistent. He is very suspicious about Blanche and her motives, and wants to see the paperwork regarding the sale of the plantation. Stanley brings up the Napoleonic code, which says that what belongs to the wife belongs to the husband, and vice versa, and therefore if Stella was swindled then Stanley was swindled as well.

Stanley raids Blanche's trunk and throws around her fox-pieces and costume jewelry, accusing Blanche of using the money from the sale of Belle Reve to pay for these fineries. Stella storms out in a huff.

Blanche comes out from the bathroom and tries to harmlessly flirt with Stanley, ignoring the clear violation of her trunk. After a few attempts at using her usual techniques, though, Blanche realizes that Stanley cannot be charmed. She switches tacks to play by his rules, and talks plainly about the loss of Belle Reve. The lawyers' papers indicate that the place was lost on a mortgage, after many generations of family mismanagement had already whittled the estate down to nothing. Still suspicious, Stanley takes the papers and declares that he will show them to a lawyer friend, but for now he is placated.

Stanley tells Blanche that Stella is expecting a baby, and she is pleased. Stella returns and takes Blanche away from the apartment so the men can have their poker night.

Analysis

Stanley and Blanche's "date with each other from the beginning" is further set up in their first significant exchange in Scene 2. Blanche is coy and flirting – Stanley will have none of that. Her defenses are already on high as she emerges from the bathroom to find her belongings strewn about, but she treats it lightly to avoid confrontation. She persists in her levity until Stanley manages to communicate that he is not going to be brushed off. But showing that her training at coquetry is nothing if not flexible, she embraces Stanley's tone and declares her intent to be straightforward and honest, to "lay her cards on the table," in an extension of the continuing poker theme. Stanley is put off by Blanche's track change – he had expected her to break under his direct pressure, but she deftly parries his advance by naming the game. "A woman's charm is fifty per cent illusion," she admits, but she still manages to diffuse Stanley by seeming to put all her cards on the table – except for the one up her sleeve. Nothing hides a truth so well as admitting to other truths.

Stanley eventually gets his hands on the legal papers, but of course he can't tell anything by looking at them himself – he came into the battle expecting that by demanding the papers he would force Blanche to admit wrongdoing, but she turned over the papers without a fight and now he has to figure out what to do with them. Meanwhile, Blanche monologues about the "epic fornications" that whittled down the DuBois family estate to its essentials – a house and a cemetery – and left Blanche and Stella's generation with nothing but death and taxes. Belle Reve was not lost to Blanche's failure, or to General Sherman, or to a shifting economy, but to a long line of indiscretions. The street-car called Desire brought the DuBois to the one called Cemeteries, and in the end that was the entire legacy Blanche's ancestors left for her.

As Blanche freely reveals this family darkness, and Stanley stares at the meaningless legal papers, Stanley loses the steam behind his accusations. Defeated, he retreats to his room with the papers, as Blanche brags to Stella that she successfully merged her "jasmine perfume" approach with Stanley's primitive directness, and has emerged the victor. Blanche is quite self-aware here – she knows that jasmine perfume alone will not save her. The blood and dirt of the Kowalskis of the world must be mixed into the solution for the jasmine perfume to last.

This scene highlights a difference between Stanley and Blanche as well as their similarity. Stanley is convinced that Blanche is perpetuating a swindle – Blanche cannot even conceive of such a thing. She comes from a social class that does not know how to make money, only how to spend it. She cannot conceive of turning a profit on the loss of Belle Reve – Stanley is projecting his own values and interests on to a woman from a very different background.

A tension between a romantic and a realistic world-view is present throughout the entire play, embodied in the contrast between Stanley and Blanche. Clearly, Blanche is the romantic – where she sees "the ghoul-haunted woodland of Weir," Stella sees simply the L&N tracks – and Stanley "no wool over this boy's eyes" Kowalski is the realist. But Williams isn't setting up a simple dichotomy, because neither Blanche nor Stanley is exactly what they think they are. Blanche's romantic worldview is as much a desire as anything else – she has seen the truth, and she chooses to ignore it. Stanley, meanwhile, believes he is seeing through the deceit and yet mistakes rhinestones for diamonds and a mortgaged old house on twenty acres for Tara. This complicated dichotomy will be present throughout the rest of the play.

Summary and Analysis of Scene 3

Scene 3

Poker night. Stanley and the boys sit around the kitchen table, swilling whiskey and playing cards. Mitch complains that he has a sick mother at home, and hides in the bathroom for awhile.

Blanche and Stella come home, too early. They are not welcome around the poker game. Mitch comes out of the bathroom and is immediately taken with Blanche, who does not fail to notice him either. The game continues and the girls gossip and listen to the radio, but Stanley is upset at the noise and makes them turn off the radio.

Mitch deals out of the hand and goes to talk to Blanche. He offers her a cigarette from a silver case with an inscription from a dead girl to whom Mitch was once attached. Blanche asks Mitch to help her hang a paper lantern, to cover the naked light bulb. They talk about her former students, and how she enjoyed watching their youthful discovery of love even if it meant that they didn't have much interest in her English curriculum.

Blanche puts the radio back on and begins to dance. Stanley storms into the bedroom and grabs the radio, throwing it out the window. Stella hollers at him, and he hits her. The men pull Stanley away to calm him down. Stella cries that she wants to leave, and Blanche leads her upstairs to Eunice's apartment.

Stanley comes to his senses and realizes that Stella is gone. He goes outside and begins bellowing his wife's name: Stell-ahhhh! Eunice comes out and tells Stanley to hush, but he continues to holler. After a moment, Stella emerges and embraces her husband. He lifts her up and carries her back into their flat.

Blanche emerges, fearful, and realizes that Stella has gone back to Stanley. She is confused and scared. Mitch appears again and she bottles up her interest in her sister's behavior to continue flirting with Mitch.

Analysis

"Poker shouldn't be played in a house with women." Mitch is adamant in his conviction that the conflict that erupts in the Kowalski household is due to the flammable combination of poker and women. It's not the card playing per se, however, that makes the situation volatile. Stanley sees himself as a man's man, with all the whiskey and cussing and misogyny he feels that implies. Poker night is a testosterone-fueled occasion, and spirits are running high and flowing fast. When the women come home, Stanley has been losing money, and needs to save face with his buddies. The combination of liquor, the late hour, the bad poker hands, and Stanley's increasing annoyance at his sister-in-law's presence all lead to him finally striking his wife.

But it is clear that this isn't the first time, nor is it the last. "It makes me so mad when he does that in front of people," Stella says, when Stanley smacks her the first time. This sentence is loaded – it doesn't make her mad that he smacks her, but that he smacks her in public. They can do what they want when they're alone, but as long as Blanche is around they will not be alone.

The reality/romantic dichotomy is further explored in this scene as Blanche spins a gossamer web for Mitch in the diffuse lantern light. She masks her age in shadow, and her own darkness in light banter. She even translates her name for Mitch as "white woods, like an orchard in spring," despite the fact that she is well past her springtime. (Anglicized, Blanche's surname is DuBoys – which she does, all too well)

Mitch is drawn to Blanche, and she to him, but for different reasons. Mitch is enraptured by Blanche's many tricks and tools of coquettish seduction, and desperate Blanche latches on to the stable and supportive idea of a husband. They share a familiarity with death - Blanche watched the older generation of her family die, and Mitch lost the girl who gave him the cigarette lighter. But Blanche's loss is more profound, more crippling, and the darkness in her quickly threatens to overwhelm the simplicity of Mitch.

The famous image from this scene – and indeed, the most famous image in the Williams canon – is Stanley Kowalski, symbol of virility and manhood, kneeling exposed and half-naked on the pavement as he desperately cries his wife's name. It is a difficult scene, in performance. Aside from avoiding the specter of Marlon Brando, the actor must also avoid the maudlin in making Stanley's desperation both sexy and terrifying. Stanley and Stella's reunion is without words – their connection is silent, physical. Stanley must likewise be a physical, commanding, dominating force in this scene, a center of gravity to attract Stella and pull her towards him, pull her down the stairs and quite literally down to his level.

To make this scene effective, the audience must be feeling exactly the same things as Blanche: a mixture of fear and curiosity. For Blanche, desire is something to be dressed up in lace and perfume and hidden from sight – it certainly exists in her life, as one of the driving forces that brought her downfall, but never as baldly and bawdily as with her sister and her brother-in-law. The only man Blanche has ever loved was her husband, but due to incompatible sexualities there could not have been any passion – Blanche has never experienced this lustful love, but only calculated lust and chaste love. It is something foreign to her, something animal, and she fears it – but is drawn to it just the same. It is an incredibly complex moment of drama, rightfully iconic.

Summary and Analysis of Scene 4

Scene 4

The morning after, Blanche fearfully returns to the apartment to find her sister luxuriating in bed. Blanche had spent the night worried sick about Stella, but the conflict of the previous night was forgotten by its participants as soon as they were back in each other's arms. Stella admits that she is rather thrilled by Stanley's violent streak, and Blanche is horrified.

Blanche attempts to convince Stella that she can get out of her situation, but Stella insists that she is not in anything she wished to get out of. Blanche doesn't really hear her, though, and brainstorms an escape plan involving wiring an old beau for money. She calls Western Union, but can't think of what to say. The focus shifts, and it becomes clear that Blanche's concern for finances is just as much for herself as for Stella – she is completely broke.

Blanche continues to try to convince Stella to leave, but Stella is firm – she is happy. It doesn't matter whether or not Blanche understands, because all that matters to Stella is her relationship with Stanley. Blanche puts a name to it – desire – and compares it to the street-car of the same name. Stella asks whether Blanche had ever ridden on that street-car, and Blanche admits that she has, that it's what brought her here. Stella tells her to stop being so superior in that case, but Blanche still thinks such emotions are the stuff of brief affairs, not a marriage and a life.

Blanche gives a speech telling her opinion of Stanley as common and animalistic, while Stella listens wearily. Stanley arrives home, unnoticed by the women, and listens in on this speech. Blanche compares Stanley to a caveman, his poker night to a party of apes, and exhorts Stella not to regress to Stanley's primitive level but to evolve into a higher level of human.

After listening to Blanche's speech, Stanley steps out and steps back in, this time making his presence known and pretending he had just arrived. In response to Blanche, Stella embraces her husband plainly. Stanley grins at Blanche as she watches.

Analysis

Scene 4 gives us the logical extension of the end of Scene 3 – the morning after, Stella is floating on a cloud of post-coital bliss, while Blanche continues with the same bluster of contradictory emotions she felt the night before. Blanche looks at Stella's situation and sees a damsel in distress, in need of rescuing, but Stella has long forgiven Stanley for his behavior. In fact, she admits that she likes his violence – when he smashed the lights with the heel of her slipper on their wedding night, it gave her a thrill.

The sisters' conversation goes round and round as Stella keeps insisting that she is happy and Blanche remains convinced that Stella is deluded. It is a troubling scene that can be played several ways – who is right? Is this domestic violence, and only Blanche is able to see that Stella is in a dangerous situation where she cannot make decisions for herself? Or is this really just the nature of the Kowalskis' relationship, and Blanche is too frigid to comprehend the couple's chemistry? The play as a whole seems to side with Stella, up until the moment Stanley crosses the line in Scene 10. For now, however, Blanche appears to be seeing what she wants to see – her baby sister mesmerized by the brutish Pollack – despite Stella's protestations.

The hypocrisy of Blanche's position is made very clear in the important dialog exchange about desire, both the concept and the street-car:

Blanche: What you are talking about is brutal desire – just – Desire! – the name of that rattle-trap street-car[…]

Stella: Haven't you ever ridden on that street-car?

Blanche: It brought me here – where I'm not wanted and where I'm ashamed to be.

Stella: Then don't you think your superior attitude is a bit out of place?

It is clear to both the audience and the characters themselves that they are discussing the streetcar Desire as a metaphor for the kind of desire that brings two people together. Each line of this exchange can be read in two ways – is Stella saying Blanche should drop her attitude as she knows she's not wanted at the Kowalskis' flat? Or that she should understand Stella's position because she too has felt crippling, damaging desire?

Blanche presents herself as a romantic throughout the play, clutching to notions of star-crossed lovers and gentlemen sweeping ladies off their feet. But when faced with a true love story, she balks. Blanche's kind of romance can't happen in the gutter. In theory, Blanche should see her sister's marriage as an epic love story between the princess and the commoner. But the truth is that Blanche's romanticism is a cover for the true cynicism of one who loves only calculatingly, for money and power and security. Of the DuBois sisters, Stella is the romantic.

Summary and Analysis of Scene 5

Scene 5

Some time later, Blanche is writing a letter to Shep Huntleigh, her former beau, threatening coquettishly to pay him a visit. Upstairs, Eunice and Steve can be heard fighting.

Stanley asks Blanche if she knows a fellow named Shaw. This Shaw is an acquaintance of Stanley's, and he claims that he knew a loose woman who used to keep rooms at a hotel called the Flamingo in Laurel. Blanche says she knows of the Flamingo by reputation and would not set foot in it, but the accusation has been made. Stanley leaves.

In a panic, Blanche asks Stella what she has heard regarding her reputation. Blanche admits that she misbehaved somewhat after the loss of Belle Reve. She feels that she is too soft and no longer attractive enough for her softness to work. Stella fixes Blanche a drink while Blanche gets sentimental – her behavior is somewhat erratic in this scene. She insists that she won't overstay her welcome at the Kowalskis, and screams when she drops a drink.

Blanche talks about her relationship with Mitch, and how she hasn't told him her real age and won't let him do more than give her a goodnight kiss. She wants to bait him into marriage, for security. Stella assures her that it will all work out, and leaves.

A paperboy stops by to take a collection, and Blanche is immediately interested. He is wary of her advances, but she is drawn to his youth, and kisses him briefly. He runs off. Mitch appears for their date, and Blanche greets him gaily.

Analysis

Blanche's deceptions begin to crumble in this scene, as Stanley reveals his investigations into her background. He comes close to an outright accusation, but chooses to instead make sure that Blanche knows that he knows, and to let her sweat while wondering exactly how much he has been told. Blanche's shadowy past has been foreshadowed since early in the play, but now we begin to see the truth about her background. Blanche is the last member of that long line of aristocrats with "epic fornications" that led so disastrously to the family's downfall. Stella escaped both the responsibility for the family's estate and the burden of its common sin, while Blanche is truly one of the family.

Blanche expresses to Stella her anxiety about her reputation – she does not want to confess, but wants to find out what Stella already knows. And, tellingly, rather than apologizing she rationalizes her behavior. In a moment of self-awareness – of seeing realistically rather than romantically – she admits that she is a soft person, not hard or self-sufficient, but with her waning attractiveness she doesn't know how much longer she can sustain the illusion. Or, in her interesting choice of words, how much longer she "can turn the trick." This choice of idiom implies that Blanche is prostituting herself – not literally, most likely, but rather that she is using her body and her charms to buy stability and comfort and association in a cruel world, and she is aware that this is a commodity with its expiration date fast approaching.

But this moment of poetic lucidity is followed by a moment of imbalance, as Blanche shows uncomfortably strong emotion for her sister and then cries out as her drink spills. Stella sees for the first time that her sister is perhaps not quite mentally stable, as her emotions ride far out of sync with the content of the exchange. The heightened unreality that will characterize the tone of the second half of the play first begins to show here. Although we do not yet hear the Varsouviana or see the shadows on the wall, the cracked inside of Blanche's mind is beginning to show from her behavior on stage.

Blanche blames her nerves on worry about her relationship with Mitch, making clear her intention to win his hand, to turn one last trick with her faded propriety and buy herself some permanent stability. Her affection for Mitch is real, but her concerns for her personal welfare and security are more real, and they drive her to manipulate Mitch into behaving as she desires.

Her intentions are undermined in the last part of the scene, before Mitch arrives, when we see a glimpse of just what it means when Blanche says she "wasn't so good the last two years or so." Culture looks more kindly on female nymphomaniacs than male – Blanche does not appear to be a predator as she flirts with the paperboy, so much as sad and pathetic. She is drawn to children, children who are innocent and gay as she imagines herself to be. Trapped emotionally in a fictional past – was her childhood so innocent with the epic fornications of her family, or her youthful love so pure with her "degenerate" husband? - she grasps at the straws of youth that she sees in the paperboy and countless other youths before him.

Summary and Analysis of Scene 6

Scene 6

Late that night, Blanche and Mitch are returning home. She apologizes for having been a poor date that evening. Mitch asks if he may kiss her goodnight – he is unsure whether she wants him to kiss her, because she has discouraged him in the past. Mitch says he does not mind her prudishness, because she is unlike any other girl he has dated.

They enter the apartment and have a drink. Mitch is awkward and uncomfortable, sweating through his shirt. They flirt and Mitch tries to embrace her, but she begs him off, rolling her eyes when he can't see her face.

She asks whether Stanley has talked to Mitch about her, and Mitch says that Stanley doesn't understand her, but he doesn't think he hates her either. Mitch changes the subject and asks Blanche her age, on behalf of his mother. She avoids the question and asks about his mother, who wants to see Mitch settled soon so he won't be lonely when she dies.

Blanche begins to reminisce about her dead husband, Allan. She was unable to fill a need for him, and shortly after the wedding she caught him with an older male friend. On the dance floor that evening, she confronted him about what she'd seen, and he ran out of the hall and shot himself in the mouth.

At the end of her speech, Mitch comforts Blanche, saying that they both need somebody and perhaps they might be that somebody for each other, and he kisses her.

Analysis

This is the only scene in the play in which we can observe that Blanche knows she is play-acting – for two brief moments, she "breaks character" and we can see her awareness of her hypocrisy and moonshine. At her own prudish behavior ,Blanche rolls her eyes, visible to the audience but not Mitch. And when she has determined that Mitch cannot speak French, she riskily asks that famous question, "Voulez-vous couches avec moi c'est soi?" - "Do you want to go to bed with me tonight?" But this scene is the first and last time she shows any awareness of playing a role, and what signifies her descent from illusion to delusion is her inability, in the last few scenes, to any longer distinguish between her game and reality

The main point of this scene is the speech about Allan and the darkness he introduced into Blanche's happy young life. The light and darkness imagery burns brightly through this speech, as Blanche compares her new love to a blinding light – something so bright that you can't actually see it at all. And this was the case with

Allan, who she loved so completely and instantly that she did not realize he was gay until it was too late.

After Blanche confronts Allan, he shoots himself. As she recounts this story, we hear the polka, the Varsouviana, from the dance hall, which was playing during the scene she remembers. We are now inside her head, and the heightened unreality of the play begins to take hold. The auditory hallucination represents her guilt and obsession, and her inability to escape the past. But we hear it too, and this shared hallucination implicates us in the disintegration of Blanche's reality.

The music stops with the gunshot – she is not just remembering but reliving, and the death of her husband stopped the music in the dance hall but also stopped the music in her life. "And then the searchlight which had been turned on the world was turned off again and never for one moment since has there been any light that's stronger than this kitchen candle." Allan's death shrouded Blanche's life in darkness, both the kind that sucks out happiness and leaves only despair, but also the kind that she hides in to avoid the flicker of the unforgiving light. She retreated into herself after this trauma, cloaking her fragile mind with shadows and delusions, and only sneaking out to find comfort in the embrace of strangers, to allow her to feel something that was alive.

Her speech also further ties together the dual themes of desire and death, but in what way? Does Allan's desire lead to his death? Or is the causal force Blanche's denial of that desire? Has she ridden the street-car named Desire to the end of its line and found no transfer except to Cemeteries, or does she reach Cemeteries precisely because she has decided to disembark from Desire?

Summary and Analysis of Scenes 7 and 8

Scene 7 and 8

Time has passed, and it is now the fall. Stella is preparing the apartment for Blanche's birthday. Stanley arrives and tells Stella that he has learned the truth about Blanche. He has been checking her background, and has discovered that she is no lily-white virgin. Blanche lived at the Flamingo, a hotel known for not interfering with its guests activities, but she was kicked out just the same when all of Laurel ran Blanche out of town on a rail for her own epic fornications. She didn't resign from the school but was fired before the term ended, because she had been dallying with a seventeen-year-old boy.

Stella doesn't believe the stories and thinks people have been telling lies. Stanley tells her they needn't expect Mitch to be coming over for birthday cake that evening – as a good friend, Stanley felt obligated to tell Mitch what he'd learned. Mitch is no longer going to marry her. And Stanley reveals that he bought a bus ticket to send Blanche back to Laurel on Tuesday.

Blanche emerges from the bathroom and sees from the looks on the Kowalskis' faces that something has happened, but neither will tell her what.

Forty-five minutes later, a dismal birthday party is wrapping up. Blanche has been stood up by Mitch. Blanche feebly tells a joke, and it falls flat. Stella criticizes Stanley's table manners, and he loses his temper, shouting that Stella has been showing him too much disrespect and calling him too many names since her sister got there. He stalks out.

Blanche tries to get Stella to tell her what happened while she was bathing, but Stella refuses. Blanche telephones Mitch, against Stella's protestations, and leaves a message. Stanley returns and embraces Stella, saying everything will be alright once Blanche has left and they can have privacy again.

Blanche hangs up the phone and watches Stella putting candles in the birthday cake, and tells her she should save them for the baby's birthdays. Stanley offers her a birthday present – a bus ticket back to Laurel. Blanche tries to smile, but cannot, and runs to the bathroom to gag.

Stella is upset at Stanley for being unnecessarily cruel – everyone has been cruel to Blanche since she was a girl, and that's what changed her. Stanley speaks of how Stella thought he was common when they met, but he pulled her out of her plantation dreams and into the dirt with him, and they were so happy until Blanche arrived. But Stella has stopped listening – the baby is coming. They leave for the hospital.

Analysis

Scene 7 is largely functional, setting in motion the action of the remainder of the play. Now all the cards are finally out on the table. The audience knows the full back story, and need only sit back and watch how it unfolds. All in all, scene 7 serves as a triggering incident for the third act of the play (in the original performance, there were intermissions after scenes 4 and 6), while further developing Stella's crumbling trust of her sister and Stanley's need to protect his wife and his friend above all else.

By keeping Blanche out of this denouement, Williams heightens the suspense of the succeeding scene. Everyone knows the truth about Blanche now – the Kowalskis, Mitch, Blanche, the audience – and all that remains is for Blanche to know that they know. In a play like Streetcar where much of the action has occurred off-stage in the past, it is an effective dramatic device to have the audience know more information than the protagonist. This device camouflages a lack of action and lends a drumming inevitability to the succeeding scenes, while elevating the meaning of everyone's actions – we know what they're thinking, and we are just as tense about it as they are. It is a technique well represented in Williams' plays, especially the ones with dead gay men (Streetcar, Cat on a Hot Tin Roof, Suddenly Last Summer, etc).

Blanche spends scene 7 in yet another one of her long baths. She says they keep her cool, but the baths are also symbolic of a fruitless attempt to wash guilt and disgust off herself. Think of Lady Macbeth's "out out damn spot" scene. For Blanche the baths are a ritual purification - and Stanley's constant interruptions of her bathing are representative of his rejection of her attempts to purify.

At the end of Scene 7 something broke, and Blanche could feel it. She sees the result immediately in Scene 8, when Mitch doesn't come to her birthday party. His absence is felt deeply by all involved, an elephantine black hole in the room. Blanche knows what has happened but cannot bring herself to acknowledge it – she telephones Mitch and worries that something has happened to him, but she knows she has been stood up. She uses the age-old technique of chattering away to avoid the conversation that is about to happen, whether she likes it or not And when Stanley leaves the room and Blanche begins to question Stella, it is clear that she also knows why she has been stood up.

Despite Blanche's deception, and despite his insistence elsewhere that Blanche is not a hero, Williams pushes the audience's sympathies towards Blanche through this scene. Stanley is right about her, of course. But the way he handles the situation is abusive and manipulative, and Blanche is clearly made to be the victim. Stanley loses his remaining sympathy when he hands the bus ticket to Blanche, committing an act of that "deliberate cruelty," the only sin Blanche cannot forgive.

But Williams then gets Blanche off the stage – it is not necessary for us to see her rage and humiliation, because we can feel it in our gut – and returns Stanley to a level of humanity in his final solo interaction with his wife. He is raging about the good old days and about being the king of his castle, but the moment he sees that something's wrong with Stella, his bluster and venom melts away. The stage direction is powerful here: "He is with her now," Williams indicates. Stanley had been off on his tangent, off in his world, but when Stella needs him he is immediately with her, completely, and Blanche is forgotten.

Summary and Analysis of Scene 9

Scene 9

A while later, Mitch arrives. They have both been drinking, and he is upset. Blanche babbles, trying to pretend this was just a normal broken date. She hears the Varsouviana playing in her head, and draws attention to the fact that the music stops after the gunshot. She avoids Mitch's attempts to get to the point, offering him a drink which he refuses on the grounds of it being Stan's liquor.

Mitch states that he has never seen Blanche in the light, that she has only ever gone out with him at night, in dimly lighted places. He tears the paper lantern off the lightbulb and stares at her in the electric light. She cries that she doesn't want realism, but magic. Mitch turns out the light and says, bitterly, that he doesn't mind her being older than he thought but he can't abide with the truth of her spotted past.

Something in her breaks at the accusations, and she admits wildly to "intimacies with strangers," which seemed to be all she was able to fill her empty heart with after Allan's death. But she'd hoped that Mitch could save her from that life. He is upset that she lied to him, and she claims that she never lied in her heart.

A Mexican woman passes outside, selling "flores para los muertos." This cracks something in her, and she begins remembering the death that brought that desire, the blood-stained sheets and the closeness of death in Belle Reve and the soldiers from the army camp who would call to her at night.

Mitch tries to embrace Blanche, to get what he'd been missing all summer. She asks him to marry her in that case, but he refuses, saying she isn't clean enough to bring in the house with his mother. She tells him to leave, before she starts shouting fire. He stares at her dumbly and she cries "Fire! Fire!" and he runs off.

Analysis

Scene 9 introduces the more fantastic elements that will heighten the reality of the remainder of the play. As Blanche becomes divorced from reality, so too does the play itself become more figurative and stagey, wearing its theatrical conventions on its sleeve. Here we have the cries of the flower seller intermingling with Blanche's memories - later it will be the lighting and sound of the rape scene, and the menacing shadows of the finale.

Scene 9 is also Blanche's last attempt at recovering her aristocratic role. The jig is up, and she knows it. But when Mitch arrives she valiantly puts on her game face and resumes her flirtatious manner. Mitch is having none of it, though – he now knows that she is wearing a mask, and he wants to see what's underneath. The moment when Mitch tears the paper lantern off the lightbulb is a shocking violation, and it mirrors the rape in the succeeding scene. He has penetrated her illusion, forcing his way into the inner sanctuary of her game. It is a harsh act, and Blanche stumbles from it as if struck. Her magic has flown away, and she is left only with hated realism.

But this light of truth is, notably, not drawn from the sun but from an electric bulb – artifice exposing artifice, like throwing a white light on a painted set. She hasn't so much been exposed to reality as to stricter scrutiny, under the terms of a different sort of artifice. But it's enough to break Blanche, and the light melts the last shreds of her façade. From there, she speaks freely, if not quite sanely, of her checkered past and the devastation she has experienced.

Her lies and pretenses, till this point, have all been for an audience. She lost Stella and Stanley in the previous scene, and now Mitch, her last audience member, has stopped watching. But the fantasies are stronger than the performer, and without any outside outlet for her games, Blanche now turns the fantasies inward. She begins to deceive herself just as she tried to deceive others, and in the process becomes less and less sane.

Like Stanley, Mitch is only comfortable when he's on the offensive – when Blanche's admission begins, he doesn't know how to respond. Her speech becomes more and more unhinged as it mingles with the cries of the Mexican woman, and Mitch just falls back and listens dumbly. When she has exhausted her story of death and despair, Mitch cannot begin to process what he just heard. Instead, he fumblingly attempts to embrace her, sticking with the "she lied to me, she's just a tramp" line that he came in with, unable to deviate from that script. Blanche is even more alone than before – she bared her soul and her words fell on uncomprehending ears. The light was supposed to allow Mitch to see her for the first time, but instead it blinded him and burned her up. No wonder she screams fire.

Summary and Analysis of Scene 10

Scene 10

Several hours later, Blanche is thoroughly drunk and playing dress-up. She imagines herself addressing her admirers. She catches a glimpse of herself in a mirror and then slams it down violently.

Stanley arrives home, also drunk. The baby won't arrive until morning, so the doctors sent Stanley home for the night. Blanche tells Stanley that she received a telegram from Shep Huntleigh, inviting her to take a cruise of the Caribbean on his yacht. Stanley plays along, for now. He's feeling amiable, and offers Blanche a beer to bury the hatchet, saying it's a red letter night for them both due to the baby and the oil millionaire.

Stanley changes into his special occasion silk pajamas that he wore on his wedding night. Blanche continues to talk about Shep Huntleigh and how he will be a gentleman, and seeks only her companionship. Beauty fades, she asserts, but intelligence and breeding do not. "How strange I should be called a destitute woman," she cries, "when I have all these treasures locked in my heart." But she has been casting her pearls before swine, she says.

Stanley's amiability begins to fade with this reference to him as swine. Blanche continues to say that Mitch returned after Stanley left, and begged for her forgiveness, but she sent him on his way. Stanley calls her on her bluff, both about Mitch and the telegram. He turns on her, shouting about her lies and tricks. His tone becomes menacing and Blanche runs to the phone to try to call Shep Huntleigh. She is terrified, by Stanley and by shadows.

Stanley comes out of the bathroom and stares at her, grinning. Blanche tries to back away from him, but that just gives him ideas. She smashes a bottle on the table and faces him. He observes that she wants some roughhouse, and he springs at her, forcing her to drop the bottle. She succumbs, and he says that they've "had this date with each other from the beginning," as he carries her to the bed.

Analysis

The director has several big choices to make in staging this scene. The biggest and most problematic is, of course, "was she asking for it?" Today, one cannot write a play in which a character "deserves" to be raped. But Streetcar was first produced in 1947, a very different time, and any production must take into account the gender politics of the play's era.

Certainly Blanche antagonizes Stanley, both throughout the play and in this fatal scene. Williams gives her plenty of chances to escape her fate here – Stanley comes home genial and happy, perfectly willing to forget his conflict with Blanche for the night. He lets it slide when she starts talking about Shep Huntleigh, though he knows it's a lie. For once in the play, Stanley isn't interested in realism – he is basking in the magic of being a new father.

But Blanche pushes him, and it is up to the director and the actors to decide just how far she pushes him. When Stanley re-enters the scene at the end, is he on the prowl and ready to strike, as Blanche suspects? Or is it only Blanche's fear of rape that puts the thought into his mind, only her defensiveness that puts him on the offense? Williams does not provide us with the answer, only with the question.

The other significant ambiguity in this scene is the extent to which Blanche has already lost her mind. This is a decision that has reverberations throughout the play. Is Blanche in control of this illusion she's presenting to the world, as it would seem when she briefly "breaks character" in Scene 6? Or has that illusion infected her brain, and can she no longer actually tell the difference between what's real and what's fantasy?

Over the course of the play, Blanche transitions from the one side to the other, from Scarlett O'Hara hiding callused hands in a gown sewn from drapery, to Norma Desmond finally ready for her close-up. But at what point does she make the switch (and how thoroughly)? In Scene 10, the director and actress must decide whether Blanche is aware that Shep Huntleigh didn't telegram and Mitch did not beg for forgiveness. Was she actually deluded, whether through liquor or encroaching insanity, into believing these stories? Or was she just desperately trying to stay in character, desperately trying to save face? Was she already losing her mind, or was it her rape by Stanley that finally unhinged her?

Who, in sum, is to blame?

Summary and Analysis of Scene 11

Scene 11

Some weeks later, Stanley is hosting another poker game. This time, he is winning.

The conversation in this scene is almost entirely small talk. Stella's baby is sleeping in the other room. Stella tells Eunice that Blanche is bathing, and that she'd been told that they made arrangements for her to rest in the country. She's gotten this mixed up in her mind with Shep Huntleigh.

Blanche emerges briefly and asks Stella to lay out her clothes. Stella admits to Eunice that she doesn't know if she did the right thing, but she "couldn't believe her story and go on living with Stanley." Eunice tells her to not ever believe it, and that life must go on.

Blanche comes out. Over at the poker game, Mitch droops at the sound of her voice, and when Stanley chastises Mitch, Blanche starts at the sound of his name. She begins to realize something is going on, but she puts it out of mind as she continues getting dressed for her trip. She talks about how she hopes she dies of eating an unwashed grape and gets buried at sea.

A doctor and a matron appear, in exaggerated institutional garb. Blanche goes to the door, expecting Shep Huntleigh, and is fearful when it isn't him. She backs into the apartment. Mitch won't look at her. The matron follows her in, and approaches sinisterly. The staging becomes less realistic as lurid shadows play on the walls and voices echo against the Varsouviana. Blanche tries to run away but the matron catches her. Stella tries to stop them but Eunice holds her back. Mitch and Stanley fight, and Mitch collapses in sobs.

The matron pinions Blanche's arms and asks the doctor if she should just a straitjacket. The doctor says only if necessary, and then removes his hat, humanizing him. He addresses Blanche directly and politely, and tells the matron to unhand her. Now calmed, Blanche allows the doctor to help her up and lead her outside. Holding on tight, she says "Whoever you are – I have always depended on the kindness of strangers." They exit.

Stella cries her sister's name as she goes. Stanley approaches his wife uncertainly, and she sobs in his arms. The poker game begins again. Curtain.

Analysis

Almost a coda, this finale is more straightforward than anything in the play. Blanche's artifice has now been entirely stripped away – she is cut down to nothing. The whole cast has gathered to witness her demise, cruelly, a going-away party to which the guest of honor has not been invited. Indeed, Blanche begins the scene off stage, once again in the bath. But now, instead of the cleansing of her own sins that the bath used to symbolize, it has become a desperate attempt to wash off the horror of Stanley's act.

This scene could easily slip into melodrama, but Williams prevents that by writing only functional and mundane dialogue. The scene is packed with small-talk – the real action occurs only in the stage directions. Even Blanche's one speech is mostly meaningless, a bit more of Blanche's poetic babble for everyone to remember her by. The speech is even conscious of its own meaninglessness – she speaks of how she wants to die from eating an unwashed grape, as unheroic and meaningless a death as one can imagine, just a bit more fluff to tide her through to the end.

The famous line in this scene is, of course, "I have always depended on the kindness of strangers." It is an ironic note. Blanche has been forced to depend on strangers - for security, for love, for comfort, for money - because her actual family could not provide. She could not have sex with her husband, so she turned to strangers. She could not support herself, as a single woman in her imaginary Old South mentality, so she turned to strangers. And when in trouble in Laurel, she first turned to her sister - and her sister turned her away. In the end, Blanche is once again sent off from her family, subject to the kindness and the mercy of persons unknown.

The real drama doesn't lie with Blanche or Stanley in this scene – their stories are complete. We have only left to see their logical conclusion. Mitch's reactions provide some fresh context - it is clear that he really did care about Blanche, and he is shamed and hurt by what transpires in this scene. He cannot bring himself to look at her, but he also can't bear to see her hurt.

But what is really of interest in the finale is Stella. She is torn between her husband and her sister, and she is very aware of the decision she has to make. If she believes that Stanley raped Blanche, then she would have to leave Stanley. If she believes that Blanche is crazy, then she has to send Blanche away. Stella seems to know, deep down, that Blanche was telling the truth. But it is finally Stella who is forced to choose magic over realism, shadow over light – desire over cemeteries. She chooses Stanley.

And so Blanche is sent off, half aware of what's happening and half willfully believing in the kindness of strangers, and Stella and Stanley are left to start their life together anew.

Suggested Essay Questions

1. A Streetcar Named Desire is laden with symbolism and metaphor. Pick one of the many recurring symbols – light, flowers, fire, bathing, meat – and trace its occurrence through the play. What does this motif add to the story and characterizations?

   An answer:

   Bathing - Blanche is constantly taking baths in the play, subconsciously trying to cleanse herself of the sins of her past. She never succeeds, however, and must return to the bath again and again. Similarly, Stanley showers after he beats his wife, and unlike Blanche he is able to come out cleansed and remorseful.
2. Elia Kazan's 1951 film adaptation of Streetcar is much lauded, but due to the Hayes Code in effect at the time a film faced much stricter censorship than a stage play. Compare the depiction of Blanche's memory of her husband in the play and in the film adaptation – how does Kazan imply Allan's homosexuality without overtly stating it? Does the film effectively convey the story of Blanche's marriage, and how does it differ from the stage script in this interpretation?

   An answer:

   The screenplay has Blanche express disgust at her husband not for being gay, but for being a poet. However, Vivien Leigh's performance makes it clear that "poet" is euphemistic, and the point gets across. It just requires a little more attention to the subtext than in the original play, which is straightforward with its account of Allan's sexuality.
3. At points throughout the play, Blanche hears the music of a polka, the song that was playing the night her husband died. Trace the occurrences of this tune and note what conclusions can be drawn about her mental state when she is hearing this music. How does it compare to the occurrences of the "blue piano" in the stage directions?

   An answer:

   The Varsouviana was the music playing at the moment of Blanche's loss of innocence, and it has been haunting her ever since. It first appears when she is actively thinking about her dead husband, but as the play progresses the tune's increased presence highlights her slipping grip on reality.
4. Two of Williams most popular plays, Streetcar and Cat on a Hot Tin Roof, have characters who are preoccupied with the memory of a loved one who committed suicide after being confronted about their homosexuality – the "dead gay man" who haunts so many of Williams' plays. Compare

Blanche's recollections of Allan with Brick's of Skipper. Can a connection be drawn between the gunshot that always ends the Varsouviana and the "click" that brings Brick peace when he drinks?

An answer:

Williams utilizes a similar device in Blanche's gunshot and Brick's click - both of these serve to dramatize characters' internal thoughts and conflicts in a way that is appropriate to the stage. They also serve as motivators for the characters - Brick is drinking his memories into oblivion, and Blanche's memories are crowing constantly into her consciousness, relieved only by death.

5. The truth is a mutating, subjective figure in Streetcar, with each of the principals having a different relationship with the idea of "truth." How does Williams express these relationships, and what role do they have on the narrative?

   An answer:

   In sum, Stanley seeks truth, Stella hides from truth, and Blanche manipulates truth. Blanche covers the truth in paper lanterns, dressing it up into what she wants it to be, and honestly believing that she has the power to bend reality to her will. Stanley's role is to peel away Blanche's layers of illusion, and Stella is caught in between, aware of lies but choosing to pick up her sister's method of dealing with reality by changing it to suit her life.
6. Streetcar is a very "New Orleans" play, closely tied to its location in space and time, while tackling universal themes and relationships. What role does New Orleans play in the work? How do the characters interact with the city, and how does the city impact the narrative? Can you imagine a production set in a different time and place? How would that change the play?

   An answer:

   You could put Streetcar in another environment of weakened economic conditions and mutating social standards, but it would be a fundamentally different play outside the Old South, and specifically New Orleans. New Orleans occupies a unique place as a bastion of old wealth and gentility while also being home to jazz, Mardi Gras, and Bourbon Street. Like Blanche, New Orleans is a faded rose fallen into hard times and cheap thrills, and this is vital to the play.
7. "I couldn't believe her story and go on living with Stanley," Stella says at the end of the play. Examine this statement – is Stella showing a remarkable self-awareness? Or perhaps self-justification? Compare Stella's behavior in the final scene to that of Stanley and Mitch.

   An answer:

Depending on the performance, Stella can be either heartlessly condemning her sister to save her own way of life, or showing that she honestly loves Stanley so much that she is incapable of disbelieving him. Her statement is wonderfully ambiguous and layered; meanwhile, Stanley sees Blanche off with good riddance, and Mitch bemoans the situation but is powerless to change it.

8. Stella and Stanley's conversation in scene seven is punctuated by Blanche singing "Paper Moon" in the bathroom. What function does the song play in the scene? What significance does this particular song have to the characters? Why do you think Williams chose to underscore this scene in the way he did?

   An answer:

   Paper Moon serves as a constant reminder to the Kowalskis of Blanche's presence in the apartment and in their lives. While living with them, she has completely invaded their existence, even punctuating their private conversations. It also adds poignance and contrast, as Stanley describes Blanche's downfall while she, unsuspecting, continues to carries on with her daily routine. The song itself is also well chosen. The chorus of "it's only a paper moon, sailing over a cardboard sea, but it wouldn't be make-believe if you believed in me" expresses Blanche's fundamental world-view that what's fake can be made real if you just pretend hard enough.
9. Clearly, a main theme of Streetcar is "desire." But does this key word refer only to physical desire, lust? What other desires are present in the story and characterizations?

   An answer:

   Although lust is the dominant form of desire in Streetcar, it is not the only one. Blanche is motivated by sexual desire but also by a rejection of the same, desiring stability and a fresh start instead. She is a character full of needs and wants, unlike Stanley and Stella who were perfectly content with their lot in life until Blanche came to town.
10. What is the relationship between sexuality and death in the play, and how does it factor into Blanche's nymphomania and fear of aging?

    An answer:

    Starting with Blanche's transfer from the Streetcar Named Desire to the Streetcar Named Cemeteries, sexuality and death are connected in the play. Those cars and the themes they symbolize run together to Blanche's final destination and ruination. Blanche's loss of innocence arose out of a death, and more deaths led to her sexual experimentation - for her, death and desire go hand in hand.

Music and Streetcar

A Streetcar Named Desire is a deeply musical work, from the strands of melody that are intertwined with the stage directions to the heroine's poetic speeches that punctuate the dialog like arias. And yet, it is a work that has notably resisted musical adaptation.

In the play itself, music plays a significant role both as a mood setter and as a source of characterization. Williams indicates a "blue piano" in the stage directions, spilling over from a nearby saloon, that comes and goes throughout the entire play. This contextualizing music is diegetic, as it exists within the narrative of the play-world as the entertainment at the Four Deuces, but because Williams closely prescribes when the blue piano should be audible it functions similarly to non-diegetic scoring. The blue piano is usually invoked in scenes of great passion; Williams states in the opening stage directions that it "expresses the spirit of the life" of Elysian Fields. It is indicated that this music should be most present in the parallel scenes of Stella's lustful reunion with Stanley in Scene 3 and Blanche's rape in Scene 9, as well as at the very beginning and end of the play, in the two moments that the Kowalskis share without Blanche in their lives.

In contrast, the Varsouviana polka is used by Williams to highlight themes of death. This music is diegetic only for Blanche – when we hear the polka, we are hearing what is inside her mind. This memory worms its way to the forefront of her consciousness when she is recalling her husband and when she feels emotionally threatened, and serves to highlight her disintegrating sanity. Like the "click" that Brick awaits while drinking in Cat On A Hot Tin Roof, Blanche must wait for the polka to play out till the gunshot that ended her husband's life before she can shake off the auditory hallucination.

Other music in the play has a more traditionally diegetic function, and even furthers the plot. Blanche's rendition of "Paper Moon" in the bath bothers Stanley while highlighting themes of illusion and belief ("but it wouldn't be make-believe if you believed in me"). And Stanley beats Stella after throwing her radio out the window.

Perhaps it is because of the strong presence of music in the plot and staging of Streetcar that it is sometimes thought of in terms of musical theater. The great theater conductor Lehman Engel, in his influential work on the Broadway musical libretto, "Words With Music," identified the emotion and pathos and passion of Streetcar as prime material for musicalization, contrasting it to the work of more cold-blooded contemporary dramatists like Albee and Pinter. Bernard Holland at the New York Times suggested that Blanche's speeches are essentially spoken arias and that the poker games are crying out to become ensemble numbers.

But both of these commentators answered their own questions as to why Streetcar is so fundamentally a straight play, despite all the musical qualities. Engel observes that characterizations in musicals, especially from the classic period, are immediate and uncomplicated. We are told who everyone is as soon as they step on stage, and the story moves forward through action alone. But Streetcar is of a class of personal history plays, like Miller's "All My Sons" and Albee's "Who's Afraid of Virginia Woolf," with an almost negligible amount of "action." The slow reveal of Blanche's character *is* the plot, and the exposition is indistinguishable from the character development. She enters unannounced, unmentioned, and we spend the next 90 minutes figuring out just who she is – and we don't really get the answer until the last few scenes of the play. And following the 1988 premiere of Andre Previn's opera of Streetcar – which did not adapt the play but rather used the original text as the libretto, setting Williams' words directly – Holland's review in the Times criticized the adaptation's characterization. The power of the play, he writes, lies in "the gradual disintegration of Blanche's outer defenses, not in sensuous arias."

But no one has commented as thoroughly and effectively on the un-musical nature of the original play as that unimpeachable source of cultural and literary commentary: "The Simpsons." The classic fourth season episode "A Streetcar Named Marge" lampoons community theater, musical adaptations of straight plays, and Streetcar itself with an extended sequence showing us clips of Marge and Flanders in a musical adaptation of Streetcar (entitled "Oh! Streetcar!," a play on "Oh! Calcutta!"), written by series composer Alf Clausen.

"Oh! Streetcar!" distorts the original play, triumphantly and hilariously. From what we see of this musical, it opens with an ensemble number denigrating "stinking rotten vomiting vile New Orleans;" provides Blanche with a standard introductory number ("I'm a faded Southern belle without a dime"); lets Ned Flanders as Stanley power-ballad his cries for Stella ("Can't you hear me yell-a? You're puttin' me through hell-a. Stella, Stell-ahhh!"); and gives Apu as the paperboy a spotlight moment ("Will this bewitching floozy seduce this humble newsie?"). In short, Oh! Streetcar! does exactly what any musical adaptation of Streetcar would do. It does not become purposely bad until the finale, which willfully distorts Blanche's departing line into a hook for an upbeat ensemble number ("a stranger's just a friend you haven't met!"), thereby assuring that the audience knows that this "musical" just doesn't get it.

"A Streetcar Named Marge" and its "Oh! Streetcar!" demonstrates just how absurd musicalizations of dramatic literature can be when they attempt to force into a different genre's contours the highly fluid complexity of a character like Blanche DuBois. Thus, even though music plays a very important role in A Streetcar Named Desire, in the end it is only a device servicing the other characterization goals of Tennessee Williams.

Author of ClassicNote and Sources

Elizabeth Weinbloom, author of ClassicNote. Completed on April 09, 2008, copyright held by GradeSaver.

Updated and revised Soman Chainani August 11, 2008. Copyright held by GradeSaver.

Williams, Tennessee. A Streetcar Named Desire and Other Plays. Ed. E. Martin Browne. New York: Penguin, 1959.

Engel, Lehman and Howard Kissel. Words with Music. New York: Applause Theatre & Cinema Books, 2006.

Kernan, Alvin. "Truth and Dramatic Mode in A Streetcar Named Desire." Modern Critical Views: Tennessee Williams. Ed. Harold Bloom. New York: Chelsea House Publishers, 1987.

Cohn, Ruby. "The Garrulous Grotesques of Tennessee Williams." Modern Critical Views: Tennessee Williams. Ed. Harold Bloom. New York: Chelsea House Publishers, 1987.

Ganz, Arthur. "A Desperate Morality." Modern Critical Views: Tennessee Williams. Ed. Harold Bloom. New York: Chelsea House Publishers, 1987.

Gussow, Mel. "Tennessee Williams is Dead at 71." New York Times. 2/26/1983

Essay: Chekhov's Influence on the Work of Tennessee Williams

by Dawn Burgess
March 23, 2003

The shape of American drama has been molded throughout the years by the advances of numerous craftsmen. Many contemporary playwrights herald the work of Anton Chekhov as some of the most influential to modern drama. Tennessee Williams has often been compared to Anton Chekhov. When asked about the influences in his life and work Tennessee Williams once said, "The Strongest influences in my life and my work are always whomever I love, Whomever I love and am with most of the time, or whomever I remember most vividly. I think that is true of everyone, don't you?" (Brainy Quote). Williams unquestionably found Chekhov's work to be memorable enough to incorporate some elements of Chekhov's style into his own plays. Through his innate sense of the human condition, Anton Chekhov served to influence the shaping of Tennessee Williams' characters in such plays as: The Glass Menagerie and A Streetcar Named Desire.

The newness of Chekhov was his portrayal of daily life and its encompassing crisis. He illustrated how the average person suffers, their imperfections, without making excuses for the characters. Interestingly, he managed to capture the way that life is a mixture of emotions. In his plays something could be awfully tragic whilst at the same time being amusing. In life like in Chekhov's work a situation that is awful would be amusing because it was ironic or because it had to be to make it through the situation. Chekhov saw this and allowed his characters to be real in this way. Characters in Chekhov's work told the story without Chekhov imposing his voice on the audience. This allowed characterization rather than plot to carry the drama.

In The Cherry Orchard the plot revolves around a woman and her family who are losing a cherry orchard that has been in the family for generations due to their lack of funds. The main character, Ranevsky, is unable to move past the problems of her history and deal with the current crisis. The plot follows her character through a very real and sincere problem and manages to combine the misery of her problem with the natural humor and irony of life. Seeing as The Glass Menagerie is a play of memories it is fitting to compare the character of Ranevsky in The Cherry Orchard to the characters in Williams' play, in particular Amanda is a reminiscent character. Streetcar Named Desire, whilst not being a play that focuses on the memories of the characters is similar to The Cherry Orchard in plot because it also has to do with losing a family estate and includes the use of wit and irony in a play that seems almost tragic.

There is a natural appeal to a writing style, such as Chekhov's where characters can be natural and still holds their entertainment appeal. "Williams himself acknowledged the influence of Chekhov [on his work] (...)" (Vannatta 79). Both playwrights share a similar attitude in regards to characterization, so much so that they face some of the same problems. There is breach between the character's feelings and their ability to verbalize these emotions. This crack can threaten to become a void, which will leave the audience lost (Stein 10). The hopelessness and the mediocrity of the characters in Williams' The Glass Menagerie as well as the characters in Chekhov's The Cherry Orchard can be summed up in this quote of Chekhov's on his plays, "Any Idiot can face a crisis-its day to day living that wears you out." (Brainy Quote).

In Williams' drama The Glass Menagerie the delivery of the actors is imperative. Realism is necessary in performance to avoid down-playing expressionist elements, much like the realism Chekhov needed from his actors to extract the essence of his meaning (Borny 101-117). To create this sense of naturalism in his writing, Williams drew from his life to create his fiction. Chekhov used this same fuel to add to his integrity as a writer. Chekhov had experiences being a physician that put him in contact with a myriad of individuals and social classes (Rayfield Preface xv and p.106).

The duality of the characters in The Glass Menagerie is a depiction of how personalities are in real life. Humans feel and act one way in an instance and another way a second later. Williams like Chekhov is capturing how humans can balance different feelings and personality traits at any one time2E People can juggle being forgiving and being angry, being hurt and laughing, being happy while crying. The beauty of the work of Chekhov and of Williams is that through their understanding of this fact they create depth to their characters that makes the more appealing to the audience.

Another famous work of Williams', A Streetcar Named Desire, bares a great resemblance to the substructure of The Cherry Orchard. Sentimentality and symbolism in Streetcar are like Chekhov's work because the staged action moves toward the conclusion negating a circuitous plot line, dealings with social themes, and the main characters are relatable human beings with recognizable problems but they are all escapists. The characters are meant to tell the story without the imposing voice of a narrator. Naturalism of actions and words, down to the natural gaps in conversation, are stressed to portray scenes in a graspable manner. (Gassner 75-77). Music is a unifying theme in both plays; it is used to carry the characters into their own dream worlds. It is used to relay themes, for instance, in Streetcar, "The love of Stanley for Stella describes precisely this rhythm of violence and reconciliation, and it exists beyond Blanche's ken. The jazz motif which alternates with polka music---in contrast to Blanche's affinity for the romantic waltz---establishes the primitive norm to which each character adapts or suffers a dissonant psychic shock." (Corrigan 84). The rhythm in each author's writing helps to propel the action. "The substructure of the story [Streetcar] has some resemblance to The Cherry Orchard, whose aristocrats were also unable to adjust to reality and were crushed by it." (Gassner 76). That sums up how the two plays are on parallel social bases and are born of Chekhov's perceived normal human forbearing.

The presence of Anton Chekhov's influence in Tennessee Williams' work is widely recognized not just in The Glass Menagerie and A Streetcar named Desire, but he held Chekhov as one of his inspirational heroes and lent his own twist on Chekhov's style throughout many of his plays. There are similarities to be drawn to that if Anton Chekhov, between Williams' characters, political/social beliefs, substructure of the stories, and symbolism. Williams saw in Chekhov an ability to truly understand and portray human nature through his revolutionary drama and wanted to emulate that unique talent. Chekhov was a master at understanding the human condition; he emphasized the human ability to be flexible and feeling on a multitude of levels. Chekhov was one of the first to pull away from the highly dramatic monologue style of acting but Williams recognized the fact that making your characters realistic and easily relatable would never be out of style.

Works Cited

Borny, Geoffrey. "The Two Glass Menageries: Reading Edition and Acting Edition" Modern Critical Interpretations: Tennessee Williams's The Glass Menagerie. Ed. Harold Bloom. New York: Chelsea House Publishers, 1988.

Brainy Quote. 20 Mar. 2001. Xplore, Inc. (parent company to all BrainyBrands) 3 Feb 2003 < http://www.brainyquote.com>.

Corrigan, Mary Ann. "Mary Ann Corrigan on Music and the Ineluctable Primitive Forces" Comprehensive Research and Study Guide: Bloom's Major Dramatists. Ed. Harold Bloom. New York: Chelsea House Publishers, 2000.

Gassner, John. "Critical Views of A Streetcar Named Desire: John Gassner on the Social Base of Private Drama" Comprehensive Research and Study Guide: Bloom's Major Dramatists. Ed. Harold Bloom. New York: Chelsea House Publishers, 2000.

Rayfield, Donald. Anton Chekhov: A Life. New York: Henry Holt and Company, 1997.

Stein, Roger B. "Catastrophe Without Violence" Modern Critical Interpretations: Tennessee Williams's The Glass Menagerie. Ed. Harold Bloom. New York: Chelsea House Publishers, 1988.

Vannatta, Dennis. Tennessee Williams: A Study of the Short Fiction. Boston: Twayne Publishers, 1988.

Essay: Morality and Immorality (The Picture of Dorian Gray and A Streetcar Named Desire)

by Nataniel Lessnick
March 01, 2003

The measure of a manâ s character is what he would do if he knew he never would be found out.

Thomas Babington

Morality is the very foundation of goodness and the pillar of righteousness. Immorality, however, is the threshold towards conspicuous malevolence. These two extremes are often but a step between which we are baffled and bemused. Morals undeniably establish the confinements of oneâ s behaviour in any given society. Should these principles crumble, ethical boundaries would give way to anarchical freedom. Both works explored in this analysis illustrate the succumbing to immoral conduct for selfish purposes. In The Picture of Dorian Gray, by Oscar Wilde, we are intrigued by a charming Englishman who discards his innocence and embraces loathsome hedonism. Tennessee Williamsâ A Streetcar Named Desire confronts us with a stout and virile figure who abides to no opposing authority than his own. Two unscrupulous characters surface from different worlds with the equivalent dismissal of moral values common to humankind. Although one is characterised by beauty and the other, by potency, they share the same vivid animation of unrestrained cruelty. It is in their ominous acts that their factual embodiment is exposed. Wilde and Williams reveal, through these depraved beings, the basis of humanityâ s intrinsic flaw: the loss of inhibitions. I will further discuss, by means of relevant characters, the yearning for moral ideals as well as the clinging onto immoral philosophies.

Oscar Wildeâ s The Picture of Dorian Gray is set during the late nineteenth century England, a period marked with the exceeding importance of social stature and personal image. The protagonist, Dorian Gray, rises as the archetype of male pulchritude and youth. His aristocracy and stunning beauty enthral his surroundings. He often poses for Basil Hallward, an artist of great talent whose art is inspired by Dorianâ s charisma. While Basilâ s most prodigious painting is in the midst of being completed, Dorian is introduced to Lord Henry Wotton, a cynical philosopher and skilful orator. Dorian is easily seduced by his manipulative tongue and his scornful theories. Wotton envisions fashioning, corrupting the vulnerable boy into an unrelenting hedonist. Through him, Dorian faces the harsh realisation that his physical attributes are ever fading. Upon this sudden insight, he dreads the physical burden of ageing. He envies the perpetual attractiveness of Basilâ s masterpiece. â ...If it were only the other way! If it were I who was to be always young, and the picture that was to grow old! For that - for that - I would give everything! Yes, there is nothing in the whole world I would not give! I would give my soul for that!â ? (Wilde p. 31). The materialisation of this wish and the metamorphosis it will ensue are to bring his demise.

Dorianâ s figure remains immaculate while the picture bears his abhorrent transformation. This is first confirmed following his amorous liaison with Sibyl Vane, an actress he meets at an infamous theatre. Like him, she is characterised by an entrancing beauty and a youthful naivety. Mesmerised by one another, they promptly exchange vows of fidelity. Dorian invites Henry and Basil to the theatre, if only to be dreadfully embarrassed by Sibylâ s artificial performance. In a fit of anger yet unknown to him, Dorian reluctantly reprimands his fiance. â â ¦You are shallow and stupid. My God! How mad I was to love you! What a fool I have been! You are nothing to me nowâ ¦â ? (Wilde p. 98). This vindictive refusal leads to her suicide. Upon returning to his dwelling, he is bewildered by a hideous discovery: his portrait had slightly altered, hinting the sinful transfiguration that would occur throughout his debauched existence.

Dorian conveys strong feelings of contrition upon learning of Sibylâ s needless death. He is conscious of his wrongdoing and feels profoundly culpable. However, Lord Henry encourages him to discard the incident and to revel in his present freedom. Dorian is torn apart as his egoism weighs heavily over his conscience. By overlooking the death he caused and indulging in pleasure, Dorian incarnates Lord Henryâ s philosophy. With the knowledge of his physical imperviousness to the aftermath of any consequence, he adopts hedonistic values. The complete denial of responsibility in Sibylâ s death is but the beginning of his moral degradation. He relishes in observing the mutilation of the picture, thus his soul. His further meetings with Henry simply magnify this descent into profligacy. â ...You were the most unspoiled creature in the whole world. Now, I donâ t know what has come over you. You talk as if you had no heart, no pity in you. It is all Harryâ s influence. I see thatâ ¦â ? (Wilde p. 120) From then on, Dorian progressively mingles with sin; provoking scandals, visiting opium dens and frequenting prostitutes.

Dorian often gazes at the painting with horror, but is unable to divert from this lifestyle, aroused by its wickedness. He is undoubtedly aware of his ethical dissipation and, despite the beautiful items in which he surrounds himself, is appalled by the ugliness of his soul. â ...He knew that he had tarnished himself, filled his mind with corruption, and given horror to his fancy; that he had been an evil influence to others, and had experienced a terrible joy in being soâ ¦â ? (Wilde p. 241) Dorianâ s fear of his predicament being discovered grows as the tableau alters with every misdeed. Although it is hidden from prying eyes, the bareness of his soul is ever-present in his mind. His hot-tempered murder of Basil not only signifies the peak of his immoral demeanour, but his obliteration of moral barriers. His iniquitous act throws him in a state of guilt-ridden paranoia. He is world-weary and borne down by the weight of this infamy.

Wildeâ s protagonist was not a villainous nor unprincipled man, simply pliable and somewhat narcissist. Under Lord Henryâ s overwhelming influence and the portraitâ s enticing protection, he succumbs to a world free of restrictions, tempted by self-gratification. When breaking apart from the moral confines that establish order, Dorian is thrust into a chaotic freedom. Without the ubiquitous prison that symbolises morality, anarchy and evilness reign, destroying the goodness in oneâ s nature. When he strikes the diabolical picture, beleaguered by remorse and maddened by regret, he wishes to purge his soul and reacquire the proper values that once governed his life. Therefore, by destroying the wantonness that marred his spirit and the guilt that plagued his conscience, he kills himself.

Lord Henry is an extremely patronizing and cynical character. His actions are not as overtly sinful as Dorianâ s, since he is not shielded from their repercussions. Although preaching hedonism, he never acts on his philosophies, remaining within the boundaries of what society deems tolerable. He thus has little knowledge of the pragmatic effects induced by his philosophy. He is portrayed as a coward, utilising Dorian to make flesh of his theories, but not venturing on them himself for fear of ruining his social figure. He is a brilliant intellect, although he has a narrow understanding of human behaviour. For instance, when he asserts : â â ¦ All crime is vulgar, just as all vulgarity is crime. It is not in you, Dorian to commit a murder...â ? (Wilde p. 234), he is entirely oblivious to Dorianâ s tragedy.

While most of humanity is constrained to moral hindrances, there are those who drift away from these ideals, and become the source of misdemeanours2E Although morality and ethics are restraining concepts, they shelter the individual and thus, mankind. Without them, there could only be degradation and self-destruction, as illustrated by Oscar Wilde in The Picture of Dorian Gray. As Mahatma Gandhi once said : â The human voice can never reach the distance that is covered by the still small voice of conscience.â ? One may enjoy life and have no fear from death if he obeys his scruples.

Tennessee Williamsâ A Streetcar Named Desire formulates a medium to reflect upon the morbid aspects of humanity and the result of these societal downfalls. Stanley Kowalski emerges from an impoverished rural setting in New Orleans as the epitome of flagrant barbarity. His speech is coarsely uneducated and his actions display instinctive crudeness. He adheres to mankindâ s most primitive rule and basic code: to hunt or be hunted. His household symbolizes his territory and anyone who menaces this tenure should be eliminated. The metaphorical episode in which he casually tosses to Stella, his wife, a bundle of bloody meat emphasises his ape-like qualities. He has little notion of courteousness, which understandably repulse his pampered sister-in-law, Blanche.

The image of a delicate flower amongst a mound of litter is comparable to Blanche Duboisâ arrival at the Kowalski household. â â ¦Her expression is of shocked disbelief. Her appearance is incongruous to this settingâ ¦â ? (Williams p. 15). She appears inherently refined and somewhat ostentatious, having seemingly never witnessed indignity. However, her false decorum is a rather deliberate effort to save herself from misery. Blanche exists in a self-fabricated universe in which she blinds herself from realityâ s bleakness. Her haughty manners contrast with Stanleyâ s uncouth behaviour and clash from their first encounter.

Stanley imposes his animalistic vigour upon Blanche since he feels threatened by her presence. He despises her aristocratic ways, her diminutive expressions concerning his origin and her dallying about with his friend Mitch. His hatred of Blanche is intensified by her unflattering dialogue with Stella. â He acts like an animal, has an animalâ s habits! Eats like one, moves like one, talks like one! Thereâ s even something - sub-human - something not quite to the stage of humanity yet!â ¦â ? (Williams p. 72). This culmination of anger is manifested in his enquiry of her promiscuous past and in his spiteful birthday gift. He relentlessly thwarts her relationship with Mitch, sabotaging her illusions of rescue. In his vile quest to bring Blancheâ s ruin, he brutally exposes her to the harshness of her position.

Stanleyâ s final effort in tarnishing Blancheâ s image is animated by chauvinism. Although his past attempts were strictly psychological blows, he now wishes to exert physical power upon her. In Blancheâ s state of vulnerability, he rapes her, devastating the remainder of her sanity. His degenerate character, first insinuated after hitting his pregnant wife, is given full evidence following this acrimonious sin. The concluding scene consists of Blanche being ostracised to an asylum and the depiction of Stanley as the dedicated husband, soothing his wife as she embraces their newborn child. The fallaciousness of this image, given what we have learned throughout the play, paradoxically brings into perspective societyâ s erroneous conception of right and wrong.

The settings of The Picture of Dorian Gray and of A Streetcar Named Desire differ immensely. Dorian is immersed in a tumultuous social environment, caught in the intricate web of social demeanour. Stanley, on the other hand, resides in a modest yet impecunious milieu. In Wildeâ s work, the innocent is poisoned, succumbing to immoral growth and subsiding into internal deterioration. In Williamsâ play, remorseless animosity is the dominating asset, as modern manâ s conduct is banished. Although these events take place at nearly a centuryâ s interval, one remaining constant is observed : the consequences on the self and on others resulting from the dismissal of morals.

Dorian and Stanley are above all human, and as every human, are subjected to the similar dilemma: to remain within the borders of moral beliefs, or to venture across into immoral conditions. The laws of ethics impose restrictions and greatly limit humankindâ s actions, but allow the worldâ s proper functioning. Both characters break free from this psychological incarceration and therefore, represent the dark side of human nature.

It is critical that we, as a community, comprehend the necessity to abide by the restraining order of morals. Only then will violence and havoc cease to exist. Is it not in our power to differentiate the good from the bad? This question lies not underneath a compulsory set of rules, but rather within the depths of our conscience. Wilde and Williams have magnified, through their enlightening characters, the step between morality and immorality. In the end, it is in our hands to decide on which to stand.

Quiz 1

1. **Tennessee Williams first big success was**
   A. *Cat on a Hot Tin Roof*
   B. *The Glass Menagerie*
   C. *The Rose Tattoo*
   D. *A Streetcar Named Desire*

2. **Williams hailed from**
   A. Alabama
   B. Baton Rouge, Louisiana
   C. Mississippi and Missouri
   D. Guyville, Tennessee

3. **Williams was greatly influenced by the mental problems of**
   A. his father, Stan
   B. his sister, Rose
   C. his brother, Thom
   D. his mother, Blanche

4. **<i>Streetcar</i> takes place in**
   A. Laurel
   B. Atlanta
   C. Stratford-on-Guy
   D. New Orleans

5. **The play is set in**
   A. the 1930s
   B. the 1940s
   C. the 1950s
   D. the 1960s

6. **The play's initial reception can only be described as**
   A. critical success and commercial failure
   B. commercial success and critical failure
   C. commercial and critical failure
   D. commercial and critical success

7. **The play starts in what season?**
   A. spring
   B. summer
   C. autumn
   D. winter

8. **The play ends in what season?**
   A. spring
   B. summer
   C. autumn
   D. winter

9. **Blanche is Stella's**
   A. sister-in-law
   B. mother
   C. cousin
   D. sister

10. **Blanche and Stella hail from a background that would best be described as**
   A. nouveau riche
   B. impoverished Southern aristocracy
   C. blue-collar
   D. middle-class

11. **Stanley comes from a background that would best be described as**
   A. nouveau riche
   B. impoverished Southern aristocracy
   C. blue-collar
   D. middle-class

12. **In the first scene, Stanley hollers at Stella and throws her a**
   A. package of bloody meat
   B. football
   C. baby
   D. dozen roses

13. **The upstairs neighbors of Stanley and Stella are**
    A. Eunice and Mitch
    B. Eunice and Steve
    C. Restus and Ellie
    D. Mitch and his mother

14. **After the loss of Belle Reve, Blanche lived in**
    A. Laurel
    B. Atlanta
    C. Corinth
    D. New Orleans

15. **The Dubois home was**
    A. a mansion called "Jamais Defonc
    B. a shack in Atlanta
    C. a mansion called "Troezen"
    D. a mansion called "Belle Reve"

16. **Stanley and his friends enjoy playing**
    A. bridge
    B. Risk
    C. horseshoes
    D. poker

17. **To calm her nerves, Blanche spends afternoons in New Orleans**
    A. drinking straight Tequila
    B. playing poker
    C. taking long baths
    D. having sex with strangers

18. **Stanley and Stella's relationship could best be described as**
    A. platonic and familiar
    B. impassionate and cold
    C. sexual and passionate
    D. intellectual, almost academic

19. **Mitch, Stanley's friend, is caring for**
A. a dying father
B. a dying mother
C. a dying dog
D. a dying wife

20. **Blanche's husband**
A. died of tuberculosis
B. committed suicide
C. ran off with another woman
D. was murdered

21. **Blanche learned that her husband was**
A. a Baptist
B. both a Baptist and homosexual
C. part Black
D. homosexual

22. **Blanche is constantly disturbed by**
A. giraffe noises she hears in her head
B. visions of Belle Reve in flames
C. visions of clowns
D. music she hears in her head

23. **Blanche worked in Laurel as a**
A. high school English teacher
B. pharmacist
C. prostitute
D. nurse

24. **Blanche's spent years caring for**
A. the dying older generation of the family
B. the lepers of the town
C. her sick sister
D. her dying husband

25. **The last few years in her home town, Blanche fought her loneliness by**

A. baking

B. becoming involved in church activities

C. helping local blacks

D. engaging in amorous encounters with strangers

Quiz 1 Answer Key

1. **(B)** <i>The Glass Menagerie</i>
2. **(C)** Mississippi and Missouri
3. **(B)** his sister, Rose
4. **(D)** New Orleans
5. **(B)** the 1940s
6. **(D)** commercial and critical success
7. **(B)** summer
8. **(C)** autumn
9. **(D)** sister
10. **(B)** impoverished Southern aristocracy
11. **(C)** blue-collar
12. **(A)** package of bloody meat
13. **(B)** Eunice and Steve
14. **(A)** Laurel
15. **(D)** a mansion called "Belle Reve"
16. **(D)** poker
17. **(C)** taking long baths
18. **(C)** sexual and passionate
19. **(B)** a dying mother
20. **(B)** committed suicide
21. **(D)** homosexual
22. **(D)** music she hears in her head
23. **(A)** high school English teacher
24. **(A)** the dying older generation of the family
25. **(D)** engaging in amorous encounters with strangers

Quiz 2

1. **Blanche lost her job back home when**
    A. her involvement in the civil rights movement angered local whites
    B. a fire, started in her oven, destroyed half the town
    C. she became involved with a teenage boy
    D. she felt her work clashed with her religious beliefs

2. **Blanche has a phobia of**
    A. getting fat
    B. being seen in direct light
    C. black people
    D. butterflies

3. **One night, after a poker game and when Stanley is quite drunk, he**
    A. beats Blanche
    B. rapes Blanche
    C. beats Eunice
    D. beats Stella

4. **Blanche is shocked after the incident of Question 28, especially because**
    A. Stella helps Stanley to do it
    B. Stanley apologizes to Blanche
    C. Stella has a miscarriage
    D. Stella stays with Stanley

5. **Blanche defends herself by**
    A. learning self-defense
    B. living in a world of illusions
    C. taking comfort in prayer
    D. going on long walks "to the movies"

6. **Blanche could best be described as**
    A. fragile and self-deceiving
    B. both tough as nails and cold and self-controlled
    C. tough as nails
    D. cold and self-controlled

7. **Blanche hopes that Mitch will**
   A. fight Stanley
   B. marry her
   C. steal Stella from Stanley
   D. kill Stanley

8. **With Mitch, Blanche always insists that she**
   A. likes Stanley
   B. is devoted to very old-fashioned ideas about sex
   C. is a communist
   D. has been beaten by Stanley

9. **One day, Stanley secretly overhears Blanche**
   A. fantasizing about him
   B. calling political contacts back in Atlanta
   C. calling him primitive and apelike and common
   D. making love to Mitch

10. **One of the important themes of the play is**
   A. the paradoxical fulfillment of prophecy
   B. the destruction of the old Southern aristocracy
   C. the balance between fate and free will
   D. the destruction of racial segregation

11. **When Mitch learns about Blanche's past, he**
   A. challenges Stanley to a duel
   B. loves her more than ever
   C. rejects her
   D. beats her up

12. **The baby starts to come**
   A. on Blanche's birthday
   B. on Stanley's birthday
   C. during a poker game
   D. the day Blanche dies

13. **Before Stella goes into labor, Blanche becomes sick when**
   A. she learns Stella is pregnant, and has hidden it from her
   B. she learns that she has tuberculosis
   C. Stanley rapes her
   D. Stanley gives her tickets to leave town

14. **That night, when Stanley and Blanche are alone,**
   A. Stanley rapes Blanche
   B. Blanche tries to kill herself
   C. Blanche hits on Stanley
   D. Stanley beats up Blanche

15. **At the end of the play, Blanche**
   A. is committed to a mental hospital
   B. leaves town, probably to become a prostitute
   C. dies
   D. returns to Atlanta to continue her work in politics

16. **Which music is NOT present in the play?**
   A. jazz trumpet
   B. The Varsouviana
   C. Paper Moon
   D. blue piano

17. **When did Blanche's husband kill himself?**
   A. After Blanche caught him with an older man
   B. After he was arrested for homosexuality
   C. After the failed wedding night
   D. After Blanche confronted him on the dance floor

18. **Why doesn't Mitch come to the birthday party?**
   A. His mother was dying
   B. Stanley told him about Blanche's sexual history
   C. He wasn't invited
   D. Stanley told him Blanche didn't want to see him any more

19. **What nationality is Stanley?**
    A. Polish and African American
    B. Polish
    C. Fourth generation American
    D. American, with Polish ancestry

20. **What subject did Blanche teach?**
    A. English
    B. Art
    C. Music
    D. Mathematics

21. **Where did Mitch get his lighter?**
    A. A jilted lover
    B. A pawn shop
    C. His mother
    D. A dying girl

22. **What is Mitch self-conscious about?**
    A. His perspiration
    B. His sexual inexperience
    C. His mother's health
    D. His bad teeth

23. **What does the Napoleonic code say?**
    A. That men automatically inherit their wife's possessions
    B. That a man and wife share each other's property
    C. That you should never invade Russia in winter
    D. That a woman cannot own property

24. **Why doesn't Stella leave Stanley?**
    A. Because she has no money
    B. Because she doesn't want to
    C. Because she has no where else to go
    D. Because she is afraid of him

25. **What makes the polka tune stop playing in Blanche's head?**

A. Liquor
B. A car backfiring
C. The memory of the gunshot
D. The flower peddler

Quiz 2 Answer Key

1. **(C)** she became involved with a teenage boy
2. **(B)** being seen in direct light
3. **(D)** beats Stella
4. **(D)** Stella stays with Stanley
5. **(B)** living in a world of illusions
6. **(A)** fragile and self-deceiving
7. **(B)** marry her
8. **(B)** is devoted to very old-fashioned ideas about sex
9. **(C)** calling him primitive and apelike and common
10. **(B)** the destruction of the old Southern aristocracy
11. **(C)** rejects her
12. **(A)** on Blanche's birthday
13. **(D)** Stanley gives her tickets to leave town
14. **(A)** Stanley rapes Blanche
15. **(A)** is committed to a mental hospital
16. **(A)** jazz trumpet
17. **(D)** After Blanche confronted him on the dance floor
18. **(B)** Stanley told him about Blanche's sexual history
19. **(D)** American, with Polish ancestry
20. **(A)** English
21. **(D)** A dying girl
22. **(A)** His perspiration
23. **(B)** That a man and wife share each other's property
24. **(B)** Because she doesn't want to
25. **(C)** The memory of the gunshot

Quiz 3

1. **Blanche always depended on**
    A. the admiration of gentlemen
    B. the prayer of the heart
    C. the strength of Belle Reve
    D. the kindness of strangers

2. **Stanley shouts "StellAHH!" because**
    A. He wants Stella to come home
    B. He is trying to scare Blanche
    C. He can't find Stella
    D. He is angry at Stella

3. **Who courted Blanche in the past?**
    A. Ashley Wilkes
    B. Shep Huntleigh
    C. Seventeen gentlemen callers
    D. Stanley's colleague

4. **What happens while Stanley is bringing Stella to the hospital?**
    A. Blanche receives a telegram from Shep Huntleigh
    B. Nothing
    C. Mitch begs for Blanche's forgiveness
    D. Blanche recieves a telegram from Shep Huntleigh and Mitch begs for Blanche's forgiveness

5. **What does Blanche ask Mitch to do for her when they first meet?**
    A. Buy her a drink
    B. Marry her
    C. Button her dress
    D. Hang a paper lantern

6. **How did Blanche and Stella's ancestors lose most of the plantation?**
    A. Gambling debts
    B. Burnt by Sherman's army
    C. Bad crops
    D. Epic fornications

7. **What is the name of the Kowalskis' apartment building?**
   A. Elysian Fields
   B. Purgatory
   C. Shadowlands
   D. Garden of Eden

8. **What game are the men playing at the end of the play?**
   A. Bowling
   B. Seven card stud
   C. Blackjack
   D. Texas Hold 'Em

9. **What is Blanche's nickname for Stella?**
   A. Stella for Star
   B. Lady Stella
   C. Stella Bella
   D. Hell's Stells

10. **Where was Stella while the DuBois family was dying?**
   A. teaching school
   B. at college
   C. In New Orleans with Stanley
   D. in Laurel, visiting Blanche

11. **"Some people rarely touch it, but it touches them often." What is Stanley referring to?**
   A. Desire
   B. Liquor
   C. Death
   D. Money

12. **Who talks about the Napoleonic code?**
   A. Stella
   B. Stanley
   C. Mitch
   D. Steve

13. **What does Blanche have in her trunk besides clothes and legal papers?**
    A. Liquor
    B. Poems from her husband
    C. Pornographic drawings
    D. Love letters from old admirers

14. **Who says: "A single girl has got to keep a firm hold on her emotions or she'll be lost."**
    A. Eunice
    B. Stella
    C. Blanche
    D. Stanley

15. **What song does Blanche sing in the bath?**
    A. The Varsouviana
    B. Blue Piano
    C. Paper Moon
    D. Toxic

16. **Why is Blanche fired from her teaching position?**
    A. She was drunk at work
    B. She had an affair with another teacher
    C. She bought liquor for a student
    D. She was romantically involved with a student

17. **What does Stanley give Blanche for her birthday?**
    A. A letter from the Laurel principal
    B. A bus ticket to Laurel
    C. Nothing
    D. A hotel room key

18. **When does Mitch come to the birthday party?**
    A. On time
    B. Two hours early
    C. Late
    D. Never

19. **Who says: "Mr. Kowalski is too busy making a pig of himself fo think of anything else"**
    A. Eunice
    B. Stella
    C. Blanche
    D. Mitch

20. **To whom does Blanche say that she always depended on the kindness of strangers?**
    A. The doctor
    B. The matron
    C. The flower seller
    D. The paper boy

21. **Why are Blanche and Stanley left alone in the apartment?**
    A. Stella is having a baby
    B. Stella is staying with Eunice
    C. Stella is visiting Blanche's doctors
    D. Stella left Stanley

22. **Who says "I don't want Stan's liquor."**
    A. Stella
    B. Blanche
    C. Mitch
    D. The paper boy

23. **Why has Mitch never seen Blanche in the light?**
    A. She is allergic to sunlight
    B. He didn't want to.
    C. He's always wearing sunglasses
    D. She will only go on dates at night

24. **Where did Shep Huntleigh make his money?**
    A. The war
    B. Cotton
    C. Banking
    D. Oil

25. **Who does Blanche get a telegram from?**
   A. Shep Huntleigh
   B. The doctor
   C. The mayor of Laurel
   D. No one

Quiz 3 Answer Key

1. **(D)** the kindness of strangers
2. **(A)** He wants Stella to come home
3. **(B)** Shep Huntleigh
4. **(B)** Nothing
5. **(D)** Hang a paper lantern
6. **(D)** Epic fornications
7. **(A)** Elysian Fields
8. **(B)** Seven card stud
9. **(A)** Stella for Star
10. **(C)** In New Orleans with Stanley
11. **(B)** Liquor
12. **(B)** Stanley
13. **(B)** Poems from her husband
14. **(C)** Blanche
15. **(C)** Paper Moon
16. **(D)** She was romantically involved with a student
17. **(B)** A bus ticket to Laurel
18. **(D)** Never
19. **(B)** Stella
20. **(A)** The doctor
21. **(A)** Stella is having a baby
22. **(C)** Mitch
23. **(D)** She will only go on dates at night
24. **(D)** Oil
25. **(D)** No one

Quiz 4

1. **how does Blanche try to defend herself, physically, from Stanley?**
   A. With her fists
   B. With a gun
   C. She doesn't
   D. With a broken bottle

2. **What game are the men starting at the end of the play?**
   A. Five card draw
   B. Seven card stud
   C. Blackjack
   D. Texas hold'em

3. **What was the state of Belle Reve?**
   A. Haunted
   B. Being rented as a hotel
   C. Mortgaged and mostly sold off
   D. Stately and grand

4. **Where were the papers regarding Belle Reve?**
   A. In Laurel
   B. In Blanche's trunk
   C. Lost
   D. At Belle Reve

5. **Where did Blanche get most of her jewels and furs?**
   A. Stolen
   B. Thrift stores
   C. Her mother
   D. Old admirers

6. **Who does Mitch live with?**
   A. His mother
   B. His sister
   C. His parents
   D. Alone

7. **Why is Mitch concerned about his mother?**
   A. She's crippled
   B. She's poor
   C. She's dying
   D. She's crazy

8. **Why is Mitch's mother worried about him?**
   A. Because he is dating Blanche
   B. Because he'll be lonely when she's dead
   C. Because he plays too much poker
   D. Because he doesn't take care of her

9. **What does Stanley throw out a window?**
   A. The iron
   B. The radio
   C. The liquor
   D. The tv

10. **What streetcars does Blanche take?**
   A. Desire and Mausoleum
   B. Desire and Cemeteries
   C. Desire and Death
   D. Desire and Sunshine

11. **Who are the poker players?**
   A. Stanley, Mitch, Frank, and Pablo
   B. Stanley, Mitch, Steve, and Pablo
   C. Stanley, Mitch, Steve, and Jorge
   D. Stanley, Mitch, Stella, and Eunice

12. **Who said "I'm not in anything I want to get out of."**
   A. Eunice
   B. Stella
   C. Blanche
   D. Stanley

13. **What did Stanley do on his wedding night?**
    A. Crashed the car
    B. Smashed the lights with Stella's shoe
    C. Threw the radio out the window
    D. Hit Stella

14. **Who does Blanche want to call for help?**
    A. Shep Huntleigh
    B. Her uncle
    C. The police
    D. Mitch

15. **Who said "Money just goes - it goes places."**
    A. Eunice
    B. Stella
    C. Blanche
    D. Stanley

16. **Who said "There are things that happen between a man and a woman in the dark that sort of make everything else seem unimportant"**
    A. Stella
    B. Blanche
    C. Stanley
    D. Mitch

17. **What does Stanley bring home in the first scene?**
    A. Liquor
    B. Flowers
    C. Meat
    D. A radio

18. **What are "flores para los muertos"?**
    A. Flowers for the dying
    B. Flowers for the lonely
    C. Flowers for the old
    D. Flowers for the dead

19. **What did the paper boy have at the drug store?**
   A. A gin and tonic
   B. A chocolate soda
   C. A sandwich
   D. A cherry soda

20. **In the play, what colors are associated with Blanche?**
   A. White and pink
   B. Blue and purple
   C. Red and black
   D. White and red

21. **How many scenes does Streetcar have?**
   A. 3
   B. 7
   C. 11
   D. 14

22. **How many settings does the play have?**
   A. One
   B. Two
   C. Four
   D. Three

23. **How many rooms does Stanley and Stella's apartment have?**
   A. One
   B. Two
   C. Four
   D. Three

24. **How does Allan kill himself?**
   A. Hanging
   B. Drove off a cliff
   C. Shot through the mouth
   D. Shot in the heart

25. **What should you always do with strangers?**

A. Get in their car

B. Depend on their kindness

C. Talk to them

D. Accept their candy

Quiz 4 Answer Key

1. **(D)** With a broken bottle
2. **(B)** Seven card stud
3. **(C)** Mortgaged and mostly sold off
4. **(B)** In Blanche's trunk
5. **(D)** Old admirers
6. **(A)** His mother
7. **(C)** She's dying
8. **(B)** Because he'll be lonely when she's dead
9. **(B)** The radio
10. **(B)** Desire and Cemeteries
11. **(B)** Stanley, Mitch, Steve, and Pablo
12. **(B)** Stella
13. **(B)** Smashed the lights with Stella's shoe
14. **(A)** Shep Huntleigh
15. **(C)** Blanche
16. **(A)** Stella
17. **(C)** Meat
18. **(D)** Flowers for the dead
19. **(D)** A cherry soda
20. **(D)** White and red
21. **(C)** 11
22. **(A)** One
23. **(B)** Two
24. **(C)** Shot through the mouth
25. **(B)** Depend on their kindness

ClassicNotes

GradeSaver™

Getting you the grade since 1999™

Other ClassicNotes from GradeSaver™

The Seagull
The Secret Life of Bees
Secret Sharer
Sense and Sensibility
A Separate Peace
Shakespeare's Sonnets
Shantaram
Siddhartha
Silas Marner
Sir Gawain and the Green Knight
Sister Carrie
Six Characters in Search of an Author
Slaughterhouse Five
Snow Falling on Cedars
The Social Contract
Something Wicked This Way Comes
Song of Roland
Song of Solomon
Sons and Lovers
The Sorrows of Young Werther
The Sound and the Fury
The Spanish Tragedy
Spring Awakening
The Stranger
A Streetcar Named Desire
The Sun Also Rises
Tale of Two Cities
The Taming of the Shrew
The Tempest
Tender is the Night
Tess of the D'Urbervilles
Their Eyes Were Watching God
Things Fall Apart
The Things They Carried
A Thousand Splendid Suns
The Threepenny Opera
Thus Spoke Zarathustra
The Time Machine
Titus Andronicus
To Build a Fire
To Kill a Mockingbird
To the Lighthouse
Treasure Island
Troilus and Cressida
Tropic of Cancer
Tropic of Capricorn
Turn of the Screw
Twelfth Night
Ulysses
Uncle Tom's Cabin
Utopia
A Very Old Man With Enormous Wings
Villette
The Visit
Volpone
Waiting for Godot
Waiting for Lefty
Walden
Washington Square
The Waste Land
Where the Red Fern Grows
White Fang
White Noise
White Teeth
Who's Afraid of Virginia Woolf
Wide Sargasso Sea
Winesburg, Ohio
The Winter's Tale
The Woman Warrior
Wordsworth's Poetical Works
Woyzeck
A Wrinkle in Time
Wuthering Heights
The Yellow Wallpaper
Yonnondio: From the Thirties

For our full list of over 250 Study Guides, Quizzes,
Sample College Application Essays, Literature Essays and E-texts, visit:

www.gradesaver.com

Printed in Great Britain
by Amazon

31315599R00059